Empire
THEATRE SHEFFIELD

Curtain up

at the Empire

Text copyright 2010© John Firminger and Dave Manvell plus reference

ISBN 9781905278374

Published by youbooks.co.uk

11 Riverside Park, Sheaf Gardens, Sheffield S2 4BB

Telephone 0114 275 7222

www.youbooks.co.uk

Printed in 2010 by Pickards.org.uk

With thanks to:

The Sheffield Star

and Sheffield Local Studies Library

for permission to use some of their images

Foreword by
Gerry Kersey
BBC Radio Sheffield

Like so many people, I have a passion for the world of entertainment. For me it is so vital in making life more pleasant. I was lucky that as a child, I was introduced to church hall concerts, which progressed very quickly to the cinema, with Saturday morning kids performances and the world of Charlie Chaplin and Flash Gordon … they ignited a fertile young imagination. Next came the real theatre. Live. Vital. And happening before my young eyes.

The first proper theatre I was taken to by my parents, was the Sheffield Empire. I can bring to mind the plush seats, rising in the different tiers right up to the 'gods'.

This is where I first encountered 'variety' Live music from solo and speciality acts. Then there was the best treat of all … .the comedy turns. Each act was given a number in the programme, which corresponded to the number in lights on the wall at either side of the stage.

It was a special feeling sitting in Mr Matchams beautifully designed Empire. Pure escape from the two up two down humdrum of Bellhouse Road.

It also endeared me to those acts which I saw with wide eyes as a kid. It was entertainment by real people … famous people.

Johnny Spitzer was the legendary manager, who although I never met him, was responsible for introducing me across the footlights to some great performers … like Jimmy Jewel and Ben Warris, Chic Murray, the wonderful Albert Modley and musical acts like Lonnie Donegan.

Nowadays, of course it's all very different. Much more spectacular for the world of television and the great pop arenas. But for me, I still have the warmest affection for the Old Empire, and other theatres like it. They live on in my mind as a reminder of what it was that kick started a lifelong passion.

Inside

the Empire

Contents

Around

the Empire Theatre

chapter one

Theatreland

A Brief History of the
Sheffield Theatres & Music Halls

Chapter One

Theatreland

A Brief History Of The Sheffield Theatres & Music Halls

According to R.E. leader, reminiscing in 1896, on Sheffield's, Theatres and Music Halls, the guardians of the town in the early 18th century were quite puritanical in granting strolling players and musicians warrants to perform in the town. There was a definite reluctance by the town fathers to welcome these strolling players to perform to the people of Sheffield. Unfortunately no records of these confrontations exist.

The Angel was a coaching inn built in 1680 and located on Angel Street, where the Argos shop now stands. R E Leader, again states this was probably Sheffield's, first theatre. According to him a handbill for Whit Monday 1761, records a musical performance there.
The Angel contained an Inn yard theatre which was built in the coach yard where coaches from many of the large towns and cities would arrive on a daily basis. The travelling players would use these services to bring their performances to the towns and cities on the coaching routes.

The Theatre Royal. Sheffield's first purpose built theatre built in 1763 and was originally called The Theatre. It was rebuilt twice eventually and was situated on the corner of Arundel Street and Tudor Street. The theatre was lost in a disastrous fire in 1935.

The Albert Hall, stood in Barker's Pool where John Lewis department store now stands.

The Hippodrome Theatre, stood on Cambridge Street just below where The Casbah now stands. The Hippodrome later became a cinema.

The Playhouse Theatre, stood on Townhead Street and previously known as Sheffield Repertory Theatre.

The Alhambra, Stood on Union Street where The Empire theatre was subsequently built..

The Angel Hotel canopy with a terracotta angel by Rossi just below the Angel Hotel sign

Around 1900 the area of West Bar, between the bottom of Snig Hill and the top of Bower Springs off Gibraltar St, there were eleven Inns and Hotels plus six Music Halls. Because of all the activity the area was known locally as 'Little Piccadilly'. For some idea of what it might have been like then, the area could be compared to how West Street is in present times.

The Surrey Theatre, Large venue located on West Bar where the Law Courts now stand and was also known as The Casino.

Fire takes it toll on the Surrey Theatre, West Bar.

The Gaiety, Gibraltar Street, West Bar, stood at side of the Salvation Army Hostel, (now apartments).

The Britannia, West Bar this theatre stood next to the old Fire Station.

The Grand Theatre, West Bar. On the corner of Spring Street and Coulson Street. Later converted to a cinema before being demolished to make way for the Bridge Street bus station

The Pack Horse, Large music hall which stood opposite The Grand between Coulson Street and Newhall Street on what became the Bridge Street Bus Station.

The Surrey, another West Bar music hall which stood at the side of The Surrey Theatre at the top of Workhouse Lane.

The Blue Boar another large West Bar inn and musical hall, located in between the Surrey Theatre and the corner of Spring Street.

Other city theatres;

The Alexandra Theatre *(pictured)* Originally called The Adelphi Circus Theatre, this theatre stood at the end of what is now Waingate, between where the Alexandra pub now stands and the bridge on Blonk Street.

The Phoenix Theatre, Langsett Road stood opposite Hillsborough Barracks.

The Palace Theatre Attercliffe Common became a nationally known venue and was previously called The Alhambra Theatre.

The Theatre Royal, Peoples's Theatre, Attercliffe stood near the bottom of Staniforth Road and Attercliffe Road and later was converted to The Regal Cinema.

The Surrey Street Music Hall *(pictured)* stood where the Central Library now stands. Some of the names who appeared there include Charles Dickens, composer Franz Litz and Italian Violinist Niccolo Paginini.

Sheffield Theatres Still Operating

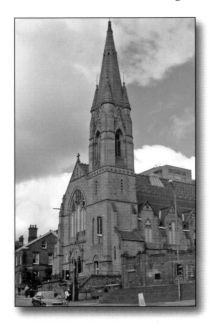

Sheffield Drama Studio, Part of Sheffield University and housed in the former Glossop Road Baptist Church and was converted into a theatre in 1970 and opened in 1971. A first class venue with a seating capacity of 200 plus two rehearsal studios and other production facilities.

The Montgomery Theatre, Surrey Street, still operating as a traditional proscenium arch theatre. It features many local productions for performances of drama, music, opera.

The Merlin Theatre , Standing in Meadow Bank Road, in Nether Edge. Founded in 1969 and built with the proceeds of a private legacy, the Merlin Theatre continues with the help of local trusts and grants.

The Lantern Theatre, Delightful Victorian Theatre located in Kenwood Park Road, Nether Edge, this is possibly one of the smallest theatres in England with a seating capacity of 84. It was originally called The Chalet Theatre and was the personal theatre of a local industrialist. However, after his death, it fell into disrepair but was restored as a working theatre in 1957 by Dilys Guite who used it almost exclusively for the Dilys Guite Players (who own and run the theatre) for the first forty years. Nowadays the theatre has been hired out by the players and used by a number of groups, bands and companies.

The Lyceum Theatre, Tudor Square, after a complete restoration this is now the pride of Sheffield and certainly rekindles the glory days of live theatre.

This list is not intended to give a comprehensive guide to the history of Sheffield's theatres.

chapter two

The Empire Palace

Charles Street

The Empire Palace, Charles Street

A Brief History up to the 1950s

Horace Edward Moss, founded a large chain of variety theatres and at the age of 25 he opened his first music hall in Edinburgh. He then went on to create the Moss Empires with his first one being built in Newcastle in 1890.

In 1895 he decided to bring an Empire to Sheffield and he engaged theatre architect Frank Matcham to design the theatre. Matcham was one of the foremost theatre architects of the day and at the time was at home designing new theatres or renovating old ones. The Empire cost £65,000 to build and had the capacity to seat 3000 people. It was built in the popular Moorish style of the time and opened on the 4th of November. The theatre was built on the site where the Alhambra Theatre had previously stood.

In 1896 the Lumiere Brothers, attracted a full house when they demonstrated their Cinematograph at the Empire, showing short films of world cities and sporting events.

All the great Music Hall acts appeared at the Empire. These included Marie Lloyd famous for singing the, The Boy I Love is Up in the Gallery, which she stole from popular singer Nellie Powers. Charles Coburn famous for singing, Two Lovely Black Eyes, and had the longest career of any music hall act. Vesta Tilley, was a very successful male

impersonator, George Formby Sr. who was the father of the uke playing George Jr. Harry Tate the impressionist and Dan Leno another very popular comedian of the day.

Music Hall Stars of the day, below left to right: Vesta Tilley, Marie Lloyd, Dan Leno

In 1901 the theatre ran into censorship trouble when French music hall comedienne **Mademoiselle Liant D'Eve** changed her costume onstage in full view of the audience several times on the first night. Added to this, one of her songs 'reached the limits of suggestiveness' and as a result a complaint was made to the Chief Constable. The lady in question was charged with gross indecency with The Empire also getting a warning that if the lady's act was not changed, action would be taken against the management. In view of this the theatre was packed the second night, although Mlle. D'Eve's act had been tempered somewhat. She changed her clothes in the wings and omitted the suggestive song, all to the disgust of the male members of the audience!

The list of acts is endless with every famous performer of Music Hall and Theatre at some point performing at the Empires; including W.C. Fields, Rob Wilton, Will Hay, Sandy Powell, Elsie & Doris Waters, Jack Buchanan, Billy Cotton, Wee Georgie Wood, Betty Driver, Al Bowly, The Mills Brothers, Frank Randle, Vera Lynn and many other favourites of yesteryear.

During the two world wars the Empire was to figure in two wartime incidents. The first one was on the 26th of September 1916 when at 10.00 pm in the southern suburbs the residents of Sheffield, heard the loud droning sound of Zeppelin engines.

It cruised into the city centre, passing over the packed Empire where **George Robey** (1869-1954) *(pictured)* the 'Prime Minister of Mirth' was performing. On hearing the drone of the engines, Robey looked up to the roof and with a

dismissive wave of his arm shouted, "Aw Shurrup!" This quelled the audience's fears and they made an calm exit of the theatre. Unfortunately the people of the East End were less fortunate and 28 lives were lost when the bombs rained down on that part of the city.

During the second world war the Empire was to be on the receiving end of the bombs. On the 12th of December 1940 the might of the German air force blitzed Sheffield. Band leader Henry Hall was topping the bill the night the bombers came. Shortly after 8 pm the intense bombardment began shaking the very foundations of the Empire. After 9 hours of bombing, the theatre had suffered serious structural damage to its right hand dome, and adjoining shop. Outside The Empire, three people were killed during the air raid who were; Norman Elliot, Sheffield Water Dept Turncock, working for the Fire Service, age 35, Stanley Slack, Fireman Aux Fire Service, age 29 and Fredrick Parkes Spencer, Police Fireman., Sheffield Police Fire Brigade, age 36. Thankfully, inside the theatre, it was the safety curtain that stopped the fire spreading. Although it wasn't due to any wartime action, The Empire suffered more damage in August 1942 when a fire broke out inside the Theatre

In July, 1944, as the war continued, a special morale-boosting **'Victory'** show was staged at The Empire with it's own souvenir programme. The celebratory production was titled 'Too Funny For Words' and featured favourite comedians Jimmy James and Nat Jackley. During the Big band era, many of the top ensembles appeared onstage at the Empire and included Bruce Stone, Roy Fox, Harry Roy, Jack Jackson and Ted Heath. Prior to the bands coming on there would be the usual three or four supporting variety acts to keep everybody entertained. Other great acts to appear at the theatre include Fats Waller who is reported to have actually wrote a song while performing in Sheffield. Another American was Teddy Brown the huge fat man who was, despite his enormity, a renowned exponent of the xylophone.

November 1944 and again in March 1945 The Empire played host the Big Top Circus and with it came a variety of different smells due to the different animals involved in the show. One was a tiger which unfortunately tore off the arm off one of the clowns. Miraculously, the poor chap sat quietly, having a cup of tea and smoking a cigarette while he was given first aid. Back in 1933 a similar tragedy happened at the Empire when another tiger had escaped and mauled a theatre attendant, and afterwards damaging some musical instruments, took refuge in a cellar. Here it fed on horse flesh until the fire brigade arrived to coax it back to its cage.

Looking back through these years, whilst The Sheffield Empire was indeed similar to many other city centre theatres, it was certainly a place with a great and eventful history of its own.

Management & Staff

The Empire Theatre was one of the many theatres owned by the London-based **Moss Empires Ltd.** whose Chairman was the influential British theatre impresario **Emile Prince Littler** (*pictured*) (Note that "Prince" was merely his name and not an honorific title) while the company's managing director was the now legendary impresario **Val Parnell**. Manager of the Sheffield venue in the early 50's was one, **Mr. Fred Neate**. Former Empire attendant and 'chucker outer',

Charles Johnson recalls the next person to take over as manager, "It was **L. E. Pierpoint**. Unfortunately, after he'd took over he collapsed and died one night on his way home from the theatre. The manager from the Attercliffe Palace came and took over till the new manager started."

The new man to take over was, without a doubt, one of the Empire's most notorious managers in its history. London-born **Johnnie Spitzer** over-saw all the shows that played at the venue along with his regular staff. He had come to the Empire in 1944 at the age of 18 as assistant manager and ten years later was made manager, being the youngest in the Moss Empire Chain to achieve the position. Artist **Colin Duffield** recalls him, "A very popular man in Sheffield, he went out for a meal with me and the wife plus the provo of Sheffield Cathedral who was dressed in his full regalia. We had a hilarious night of food, drinking and dancing. He (Johnnie) carried around a portable radio which he would sit and listen to where ever he was." When not at work Mr. Spitzer resided a few hundred yards up the road from the Empire in his own suite at The Grand Hotel. Johnny had a 'special rate' with the hotel although as **Colin Duffield** recalled Johnnie's 'suite' "it wasn't much bigger than a broom cupboard." Confining the room even more was a huge stack of newspapers by his bed. Someone else who became a close friend of Johnnie's was **Eric Kalman**. "I was one of the crowd who congregated in the Grand Hotel and slowly we became friends." Johnnie Spitzer, Star reporter and Eric Kalman (*pictured far right*). However, as Eric remembers, Johnnie was not always that easy to become friends with as he could be quite insulting towards others. "He called me Fritz because I was German, but I was an easy-going type and that's why we got on so well. I thought the world of Johnnie." Despite Johnnie's sometimes unsociable

demeanour, he was the person that everyone wanted to know, "he had an aura about him" Eric continues, "He was pulling the audiences in and could get whichever act he wanted." Others who were attracted by Johnnie's charisma were Editors of the Star who'd hold parties for him up on the top floor of the Star's York Street offices. Also because of Johnnie's size, he couldn't drive so Eric became his chauffeur, "I used to take him everywhere" Eric recalls one of their regular trips down to the Locarno Ballroom. "I had Johnnie Spitzer sitting behind me with orchestra leader Bert Ambrose in the back, and the third person was Max Bacon, the heavyweight comedian. My little car was a Ford Prefect and I had to try and counter-balance the weight and really drive slowly as it was nearly down to the road!".

14

Maureen Burrows worked at Cole Brothers (then at Coles' Corner) where Johnnie was a regular customer, "Every Friday Johnnie brought the top act into Cole Brothers for lunch! The artists were very smart; men in suits and the women very dressy!."

Another place that Johnnie called in was Boots The Chemist as former staff member **June Kirkland** remembered. "Mr. Cross was the manager of Boots and was a big friend of Johnnie's. When any stars were staying at the Grand Hotel he always brought them into Boots. All the old girls will remember this. I can remember Lana Morris, Frankie Vaughan, Ann Shelton and Violet Pretty to name a few."

It's also interesting to note that on one or two occasions Johnnie was credited in the programme as the arranger for the orchestra's selection of 'Tunes Of The Day'.

At 24 stone Johnny was quite a larger than life character with an enormous appetite for food and women. Orchestra leader Maurice Newton once walked into Johnnie's office to find him eating a large pork pie. Because of Johnnie's Jewish upbringing Maurice remarked that thought it was against Johnnie's religion to eat a pork pie, to which Johnnie grinned and simply said "My only God is food"! Other members of the staff wondered what would happened when London manager Val Parnell paid Johnnie a visit and found him eating one of his enormous meals in his office. Their curiosity was soon dispelled when one of the staff walked into Johnnie's office and found him and Val enjoying a meal together whilst watching television! However Johnnie never touched alcohol as **Eric Kalman** recalls, "I never saw Johnnie drink alcohol. He drank gallons and gallons of water and milk and he sweated profusely, it just ran down his face." Described as a ladies' man, his size and sweating made him not always attractive to women although, because of his fame, some women would still be drawn to him. Johnnie lived at the Grand Hotel for seventeen years and after the Empire closed he stayed on working for a London Impresario. When the Empire closed, he took a memento of the old theatre with him being, the curtains from his office, which he'd bought in an auction for £2.2s.0d. (£2.10p). As the good life got the better of him he collapsed and died in his hotel room in January 1971 at just 44 years of age. **Eric Kalman**; "He was on the phone in his room, he just dropped dead. We couldn't believe it, I was told by one of the lads." A reflection of his popularity was the 500 people who attended his funeral with a special bus service put on. Just like his beloved Empire, The Grand Hotel was demolished two years later.

Despite his popularity, Johnnie was a lonely man. **Eric Kallman**, "He was an enigmatic man, a contradiction in terms, but he was well thought of by Moss Empires."

Johnny Spitzer enjoys a meal in his office

Many of the Empire shows were of course made up of touring variety bills and/or complete touring productions. The week's run of shows would generally begin on Monday and would be split into two houses, the first one at 6.15pm and the second one at 8.30pm. The shows themselves would also be split into two halves separated by an interval so the artistes generally worked hard for their wages, especially the different dance acts who would usually open each show and re-appear at least once again during the night. There was a barring clause for artists that, if you appeared at the Empire, you could not appear at another theatre within a 30 mile radius for 4 weeks before and after your date at the Empire although probably not always adhered to.

As radio presenter **Gerry Kersey** fondly recalls "this was the first theatre that I was ever entertained in." He also remembers how The Empire shows ran in correspondence with the number of the acts as listed in programme. "I've got this memory of these lights at either side of the stage that showed a number and the number referred to the acts." As a young ventriloquist **Ray Alan** recalls the dressing room arrangements, "those acts on the bottom of the bill, their dressing rooms were the furthest from the stage and those at the top of the bill was at the side of the stage, or nearby." In view of his billing, Ray remembered that his dressing room was up three flights of stairs.

On each of the floors, Pit, Circle and Gallery the attendants' job was to shout to the bar staff so they could man the bars ready for serving. In the Gallery, there was a bar which served both soft and alcoholic drinks. Just prior to the interval to, the manager was obliged to stand out front in white tie and tails, without the top hat.

For many Sheffielders, a night out at The Empire would be of course a special occasion and just sitting inside the theatre would be part of the magic, enjoying the grand splendour of it all.

Although there had probably been many onstage, in terms of audience response, during the 50's there were two deaths in the theatre when members of the audience had collapsed and died. In case of such occurrences and any other mishaps, the St. John's Ambulance Service were always in attendance inside the theatre. There was also a night Fireman as **Charles Johnson** remembers, "He had to check every ashtray in the back of the seats to check for any burning embers."

There would be two shows a night with the first house at 6.00 and the second house at 8.30. There would also be afternoon Matinees on Saturday The box-office would be open from 10.00am until 9.00pm and ticket prices ranging from 1/3 (6p) up in the Gallery through to the Boxes priced at 35/- (£1.75p).

Charles Johnson recalls, "If a particular show wasn't doing well, two complimentary tickets were given away. On the other hand, if it was a sell-out, no comps. were available."

On duty outside the front entrance would be the commissionaire, dressed in his smart, decorative uniform. In this capacity, he was quite an important person, controlling the crowds of people who went in. Although he would often be heard proclaiming a 'full house', if you were to give him half-a-crown, (2/6 or twelve and a half pence in todays world), he'd find you a couple of seats.

A Sheffield tramcar advertising the Empire Theatre.

An intermission drink advertisement

Ice Cream advertisement

Strike Up The Band

The Empire Orchestra

As on all the shows, the **Empire Orchestra**, under the direction of **Maurice Newton,** *(pictured right)* would start the programme off with the Overture and would accompany all the performers (when required) and play during the interval with a varied selection of popular pieces and well known classics. A well respected violinist, Maurice was the Musical Director at the Empire from 1943 right up to its closure in 1959. He began his professional career as a violinist at the age of sixteen, billed as Master Newton. During the 1st, World War he conducted an orchestra at the Wharncliffe Hospital, entertaining the wounded. He served with the Army himself in France and was wounded at Passchendaele in 1917. The next year he was out in Russia entertaining the troops and travelled around by reindeer slay.

Back home in 'civvy street' Maurice played in a number of Sheffield cinemas and theatres as well as touring with dance orchestras as well as playing summer seasons at coastal resorts. Conducting the Empire Orchestral Maurice would always be immaculate in swallow tails and bow-tie. He's remembered for his light hearted approach to his job which was a great assurance to many of those young artistes who appeared at the Empire. At the Empire the overture would begin the variety shows and as his small prompting light changed from red to green Maurice and the orchestra would open up with either "Theatreland" or his own

composition "Good Evening". Many people also recall Maurice for his great courtesy and his "Newtonian" smile whilst seeing him singing along as he conducted the orchestra. In the intermission Maurice and the orchestra would return to play as some of the audience sat and listened whilst others went to the theatre bars. At the end of each show the Maurice would conduct the Orchestra as they would play the audiences out with their usual closing piece, "Cheerio". As he contributed much to the shows' continuity, Maurice was held in high esteem by his fellow musicians and artistes alike. Some of the musicians who made up the Empire Orchestra are also remembered for their efforts going on to teach some of the young up and coming musicians around the city. One member, a trumpeter is remembered for coming to work on his red push-bike. In those days, it was custom for the performers to tip the orchestra when they collected their music sheets at the end of the week. If anyone failed to give a tip, they'd often find on their next visit to the theatre that their music had been written on with whole bars crossed out in pencil, and replaced with added instructions! Hence, the music would be virtually unusable at the next theatre and proved to be quite costly for the more meaner performers.

Overture; Maurice conducts the Empire Orchestra

On The Street

With The Empire in pride of place, we take a nostalgic look back around the area where it stood

As with most theatres, the original front façade of The Empire Theatre looked quite impressive with it's two domes towering above the roof almost resembling something from an 'Arabian Knights' setting. Its imposing frontage took up the whole of the top part of Charles Street, on the left-hand side between Pinstone Street and Union Street. Like many of the buildings in the city centre, The Empire had also suffered some damage from the Second. World War and through the 50's only one of he domes remained. The bottom shop on the corner of Charles and Union Street had also been damaged and similarly, the top corner of Charles St. and The Moor was where the theatre's sweet shop had previously stood. Afterwards these two areas were cordoned off with large advertising hoardings. Other advertising for the Empire's various shows would be seen in a number of display cases around the front entrance sporting eye-catching posters and photographs of some of the star performers inside them. A large glass canopy hung over the theatre's front entrance, which had replaced a smaller facade and other exit doors were situated around the building.

As to be expected the area in which the theatre was located would generally be (as it still is) in a busy part of town. Union Street in particular always seemed busy especially during theatre opening times with queues on either side of the road. This would be due to the fact that opposite the Empire was of course the Palace, one of the city-centre's popular cinema houses with a capacity of 1000.

Queues would also form down the side of The Empire along Union Street and round to the main entrance on Charles Street eagerly waiting to get in for the nightly shows. Some nights this would also attract various street entertainers who would either be singing or playing a

musical instrument whilst going along the queues with a collection cup. Also situated about halfway down the Empire building was the theatre's stage-door where crowds would often gather before and after a show, depending who was performing in the hope of maybe getting an autograph or simply a glimpse of the star attraction.

Just above The Palace cinema was the Phoenix Hotel, known as Ted Ross's, after the Landlord. This was where some of the Empire's musicians and performers could conveniently nip across for a quick pint when not required during the shows.

Another near-by pub was the Red Lion, on Charles Street which had a concert room adjoining the bar and was called the Palace of Varieties. It is said that in Victorian times performers from the Empire would nip round and give impromptu performances here.

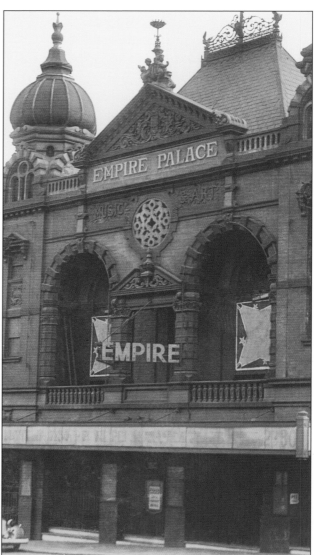

Pinstone Street and the corner of Charles Street, Sheffield

Front of the Empire on Charles Street

Situated just a few yards away up on the corner of Norfolk Street and Charles Street was the car showroom of Brook Shaw's the Ford dealer. After being damaged in the war, it became a single storey building and boasted large windows. Next door to the Empire was the infamous El Mambo coffee bar. In the 1950's this was a place that had something of an unsavoury reputation, due to the various types of clientele who frequented there. Indeed I (John Firminger) can recall my parents warning me never to go in the place because some of the people in there were *'not very nice'*. However all I can seem to recall of the El Mambo is that both the style of clothes of some of those inside contributed to a seemingly exotic atmosphere, although I only ever deduced this from the outside. **Judd Newton** "You could go upstairs or downstairs. Downstairs was where the jukebox was." The 'Mambo was subsequently turned into a more homogenised coffee-bar and re-named The Copper Coin.

Next to The El Mambo was the Cambridge Arcade with various shops inside including a newsagent, jewellers, hairdressers, SUT (Sheffield United Tours) booking office. This would lead up through to Pinstone Street where a shabby-looking blind man would be a familiar sight selling his meagre wares of packets of lavender and matches. At the top, the renowned Sheffield tailor Barney Goodman stood across the arcade from Suggs' Sports Shop.

One of the workers working on the construction of the near-by Goodwin Fountain was former DJ **Gaspin' Gus**

Teenager's Favourite
Dickie Valentine

Chapman who recalls often seeing some of the performers on their way to The Empire. "The comedian Arthur Haynes would walk past in his white raincoat and always say 'Morning', whilst David Whitfield simply drove past in his limo and totally ignored us." Also passing by, Gus received some healthy advice from trumpeter **Eddie Calvert**, "He saw me with a cigarette and told me I'd be better off if I stopped smoking."

THE HAIR STYLISTS • ARTISTS IN HAIR COLOURING

Maison Constance
TEL. 28707
62/64 CAMBRIDGE ST. MOORHEAD

Located just up the road from the Empire on Pinstone Street, opposite the Peace Gardens, was The Teenage Tavern, which situated in the basement of Marsden's Milk Bar. Aimed obviously at a younger clientele, it had been opened by Dickie Valentine the popular star of stage, television and records and one of Britain's early pop idols.

Teenage Tavern

Before the show why not meet your friends in the "Tavern" at Marsden's Milk Bar (opposite the Town Hall) All the stars are there to sing for you

— TEENAGE TIME IS TAVERN TIME —

At the opening ceremony, manager of the Milk Bar Mr. Horace Lyles asked Dickie to autograph a five pound note. As this was roughly half of week's wage back then, such frivolity amazed all those attending, including Dickie Valentine! As it was intended, the Teenage Tavern was very popular with teenagers of the time, highlighting the popularity of coffee bars and jukeboxes. Many of the youngsters would start their nights entertainment at the Tavern, before going on to see some of the more teen-oriented shows at the Empire. Saturday afternoons were another popular time-slot for teenagers congregating there, drinking endless cups of coffee and listening to the vibrant sounds of rock'n'roll pulsating from the jukebox.

Whilst most of the star names stayed at the Grand Hotel during their engagement at the Empire, the supporting acts would usually be booked in at theatrical digs in St. Mary's Road, located about a three quarters of a mile from the theatre.

Back in these times Sheffield was still a somewhat grimy city due to it's heavy industry, yet places such as The Empire Theatre and those who appeared there certainly gave it some sparkle that will hopefully continue to shine through the pages of this book.

The Empire Strikes Back
A Personal Recollection By John Firminger

An inside view of the Empire Theatre, showing the stalls, circle and the Gods.

My first trip to the Empire Theatre is still pretty vivid in my mind, even after nearly sixty years. Accompanied by my Mum, I must have been about seven or eight and the show we went to see starred the American singing cowboy Tex Ritter and of course a hero of all schoolboys like myself. We had seats booked up in the top balcony, commonly known as the 'Gods' due to how far up they were in the building and it certainly seemed like a long climb up the stairs. Compared to the more plush red velvet upholstery of the lower seating areas the wooden rows were quite basic.

Unfortunately as soon we found our seats I found myself gripped with fear as we looked down towards the stage. The rows of seating were so steep they seemed like (to me) almost vertical and looking down the stage seemed to be so far down. In hindsight, I suppose this could have been my first experience of suffering from vertigo although I managed to overcome it later in life. Panic stricken and sitting there in the dark, I can recall that I just couldn't settle in my seat and pleaded with my Mother for us to go down stairs and to the safety of the stalls. What also made it seem more scary was the fact that, going up or down the steps, the gap between the steps was like the equivalent of two steps. Very reluctantly my Mom relented and took me downstairs where she had to pay extra for the more luxurious (and seemingly safer) seats in the stalls, something that she was obviously not too pleased about at all. Although I felt a great deal of relief, I also felt quite bad that I'd inconvenienced my mother in this way.

After the show I joined the queue outside the stage-door to get Tex's autograph and as I approached him I noticed how tanned he looked. I thought this must be because he was an American cowboy and that's how they all looked. Little did I realise this was because he'd still got his stage make-up on! I didn't return to The Empire for something like two years later, when, along with some of my school-pals, we went to see the upcoming female singing star Shirley Bassey. By now my fear of heights had subsided, although we watched the show from the relative safety of the safety rail on the front row of the balcony.

It's many years now after my last visit to The Empire and in that time I have developed a complete fascination with Sheffield's past, especially on the entertainment side. When Dave Manvell showed me his collection of original programmes from The Empire Theatre it also transported me back mentally to my childhood days of the 50's too. Including many of the names who appeared at the Empire during those years Pop singers, novelty acts, acrobats, speciality acts, jugglers and comedians were all featured in the numerous variety bills listed in these programmes.

Fascinated by this veritable treasure-chest of information within these pages, Dave and myself were suitably enthused and thought it would be a good idea to put together a book based round these, and subsequently other programmes we have discovered. Reproducing the programme pages, they display the many shows and productions. Reflecting the passing years along with the various developments in the entertainment field by way of the different types of acts that were being booked into The Empire. Some of the programmes' original adverts are also included to hopefully evoke some of the flavour and more memories of those times. Although by no means a complete list, the information is also accompanied by pictures and other related archive material. Many of the names included here will be almost forgotten despite them being household names during the 50's and 60's and this book will also serve as a reminder of them. To add further interest we have also included the recollections of various people with their own memories of the Empire. So, take your seats for what we hope will be a pleasurable and entertaining trip back to some of Sheffield's and Showbiz's past.

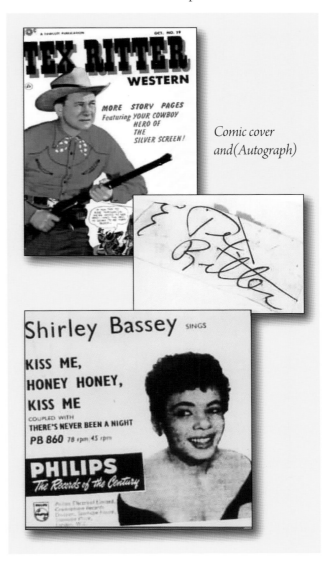

Comic cover and (Autograph)

Frankie Vaughan appeared on many occasions at the Sheffield Empire

Empire
THEATRE SHEFFIELD

chapter three

The Lost Programmes

Chapter Three

The Lost Programmes

Dave Manvell recalls how his discovery of Sheffield's past led to this book and other treasures

On one of my eternal quests to find long lost artefacts of Sheffield's past, my attention was drawn to a bundle of programmes in a local antiques centre. Initially I thought they were football programmes but on further inspection I realised they were in fact original programmes from Sheffield's Empire Theatre, and all dating back to the 1950's.

As I gingerly opened one of them and looked at the contents, I was immediately transported back to my childhood of the 50's. Although I had never actually been to the Empire, as a child, these programmes did however contain the names of many of my childhood TV heroes. Some of the names had already enjoyed success, whilst others were still up-and-coming while others were relegated to doing the rounds of similar theatres before disappearing into obscurity or making the transition to another form of entertainment. Some of the up-and-coming names would also go onto find new success as actors, game-show hosts and prominent figures within the various aspects of the entertainment industry. There was the ventriloquist Saveen and his doll Daisy May, the Morton Fraser Harmonica Gang and Charlie Chester whose show we watched sitting around the TV on a Saturday evening. They were all there.

That was it; without any doubt I knew I had to purchase this unique and historic collection of programmes from Sheffield's past.

Shortly after I showed these to my good friend and fellow local history enthusiast John Firminger, who was just as enthralled with them as I was. With these programmes we knew we had the beginnings of a book, and, as they say, the rest is history, well it most certainly was in fact, right there in the pages of those programmes!

As a follow onto this Martin Dawes, of The Star, wrote an article in the paper entitled The Days of Empire and included a mention of us working on this book, with a memo to us; 'Don't forget the tigers!' (to find out the answer to that one you will have to read the book).

From the first article came a second one with also an invitation for any readers to get in touch with us with any memories of The Empire. This resulted with the initial lost programmes growing from forty to just under a hundred with the help of Star, readers Eric Kalman and Judd Newton. Another very useful contact was Charles Johnson and his daughter Ann Chesney who had a wonderful collection of original autographs and signed photos of many of the stars who appeared at the Empire. As we discovered, Eric Kalman was a close friend of the Empire's legendary manager Johnny Spitzer and Judd was in fact the nephew of the Empire's musical director Maurice Newton whilst Charles Johnson was also a former attendant at the Empire who spoke to many of the performers.

Added to the forty programmes I originally discovered, Eric kindly loaned us another sixty with a further five coming from Judd plus five more from another former patron of The Empire, Margaret Hobson, all of which were different and now gave us over one hundred to draw the information from.

Thanks to these and other people's reminiscences and memorabilia, we certainly now had a greater wealth of material regarding some of Sheffield's showbiz history of the 1950's. We hope you enjoy the contents of these 'lost' programmes and other recollections of those times which we're really happy to be able to share with you.

24

The Programmes

PROGRAMME
for week commencing MONDAY, OCT. 27th, 1952

JACK HYLTON & CHESNEY ALLEN
(For Garrirights Limited)
present a Fun Frolic

OPEN THE CAGE
Produced by Charles King

1. You Can't Help Laughing at—
   BRIAN KENT, EILEEN ROGAN GIRLS, DONOVAN & HAYES, VIKING TRIO & CHARMAINE, THE TWO PLAYBOYS, PEGGY POWELL, MAUREEN ROSE,
   EDDIE GRAY & ARTHUR ENGLISH

2. The Assassination of Sorrow   -   -   -   DONOVAN & HAYES

3. Flogging the Hoops -   **ARTHUR ENGLISH & EDDIE GRAY**

4. A Cycling Rodeo   -   -   -   -   THE THREE ASTONS

5. ??????   -   -   -   -   -   -   ??????

6. Rainbow Ballet   -   BRIAN KENT, MAUREEN ROSE, and THE GIRLS

7. Open the Cage—Here he Comes   -   **ARTHUR ENGLISH**

8. A Little Bit of Scotch—Down in the Glen with
   MAUREEN ROSE, BRIAN KENT,
   THE EILEEN ROGAN GIRLS AND COMPANY
   Piper: JOHN CAMPBELL

INTERMISSION
THE EMPIRE ORCHESTRA
Under the direction of MAURICE NEWTON

FULLY LICENSED BARS IN ALL PARTS OF THE THEATRE
Favourite proprietary brands at Popular Prices
Whisky 2/-   Gin 1/9   Port and Sherry 2/-
Beers and Minerals at moderate prices

Programme continued overleaf

PROGRAMME
Continued

9. Our Girls, in Gold and Silver

10. Fun and Music   -   -   -   -   THE TWO PLAYBOYS

11. French as She is Not Spoke   -   "Monsewer" EDDIE GRAY

12. The Cabin in the Pines, featuring the Rage of the Country—
    THE BUTLIN AMERICAN SQUARE DANCERS
    Ace Caller: PEGGY POWELL

    Miss Powell sings the numbers from "Annie Get Your Gun" by kind permission of Emile Littler

13. A Rhapsody of Movement
    THE VIKING TRIO & CHARMAINE
    and THE EILEEN ROGAN GIRLS
    Singers: BRIAN KENT & MAUREEN ROSE

14. "Antimacassars and Old Laces" (A dramatic episode of the year 1884)
    Compere -   -   -   -   -   STAN KEWLEY
    Benjamin -   -   -   -   -   BRIAN KENT
    Dorcas   -   -   -   -   -   PEGGY POWELL

15. Finale -   -   -   -   -   -   THE COMPANY

Scenery designed, painted and constructed by Keystudios Ltd. Costumes designed and executed by Dukes of Wardour Street. Nylons by Kayser-Bondor. Shoes by Gamba Ltd. Cigarettes by Abdulla. Lighting equipment by the Strand Electric Co. Ltd. Ladies' Handbags Sidney Russell. Mr. Arthur English's ties by Ivy (his wife).

Stage Director and Manager ...... } For { .... DANDY PAGE
Musical Director .... } GARRIRIGHTS { .... WILFRED GREEN
Publicity .... } LTD. { .... ROBERT SWASH

The Management reserves the right to refuse admission to the Theatre, and to change, vary or omit, without previous notice, any item of the programme

PROGRAMME
for week commencing MONDAY, SEPT. 29th, 1952

1. OVERTURE   -   -   *The Empire Orchestra*

2. GERALDINE & JOY   -   -   *Rhythm Rhapsody*

3. JOY JACKLEY & SETH JEE   *A Fool and her Fancy*

4. TRIO NAJARROS   *Eccentric Continental Acrobats*

5. "DAISY MAY"   -   -   *The Captivating Starlet*
   Assisted by SAVEEN

6. HALL, NORMAN & LADD   -   *Almost Musicians*

INTERMISSION
Selection   -   "SOUTH PACIFIC"   -   Richard Rodgers
THE EMPIRE ORCHESTRA
Under the direction of MAURICE NEWTON

Programme continued overleaf

PROGRAMME
Continued

7. GERALDINE & JOY   -   -   *Entertain Again*

8. JOY JACKLEY & SETH JEE   -   *Happy Go Lucky*

9. BERYL ORDE   -   -   *Radio's Popular Impressionist*

10. THE DEEP RIVER BOYS
    Sepia Harmony Team from U.S.A.

The Management reserves the right to refuse admission to the Theatre, and to change, vary or omit, without previous notice, any item of the programme

The Programmes

PROGRAMME

for week commencing MONDAY, 30th AUGUST, 1954

1. OVERTURE - - *The Empire Orchestra*

2. THE ROYBELLES

3. THE KEN DORVILLES - *Novelty Act*

4. IRIS SADLER - - *Saucy but Nice*

5. THE SKYLONS - - *Aerial Thrills*

6. THE ROYBELLES

7. HARRY SECOMBE *The Golden-voiced Comedian from the "Goon Show" and "Educating Archie"*

INTERMISSION
Selection - "Kiss Me Kate" - Cole Porter
THE EMPIRE ORCHESTRA
Under the direction of MAURICE NEWTON

FULLY LICENSED BARS IN ALL PARTS OF THE THEATRE
Favourite proprietary brands at Popular Prices
Whisky 2/- Gin 1/9 Port and Sherry 2/-
Beers and Minerals at moderate prices

Programme continued overleaf

PROGRAMME
Continued

8. ROYBELLES

9. IRIS SADLER - - *Astrology with a Laugh*
Assisted by Allen Johns

10. "The Mad Musician"
DR. CROCK AND HIS CRACKPOTS

Billie Campbell	Song Plugger
Charlie Rossi	Wee Crackpot
Willie O'Leary	Potty
Ken Grieff	Trumpet Blower
Rex Eaton	The Man in Black
Ted Fielding	Percussion Perhaps
Larry Jay	The Quiet One

Jimmy McKnight and his Electronic Organ and other members of Crock's Academy

---

PLEASE NOTE—PHOTOGRAPHING IN THE THEATRE IS FORBIDDEN

PROGRAMME

for week commencing MONDAY, MAY 11th, 1953

Bernard Delfont
presents

ROCKIN' IN RHYTHM

1. OVERTURE - - *The Empire Orchestra*

2. CONWAY & DAY *Introduction to the Dance*

3. GEORGE MEATON
"The Big Noise"
assisted by Marianne

4. TED & GEORGE DURANTE - *Acrobatics*

5. JOE CHURCH - *Something New in Comedy*

6. TOMMY FIELDS
The Popular Singing Comedian

INTERMISSION
Overture - "A MAY DAY" - Haydn Wood
THE EMPIRE ORCHESTRA
Under the direction of MAURICE NEWTON

FULLY LICENSED BARS IN ALL PARTS OF THE THEATRE
Favourite proprietary brands at Popular Prices
Whisky 2/- Gin 1/9 Port and Sherry 2/-
Beers and Minerals at moderate prices

Programme continued overleaf

PROGRAMME
Continued

7. CONWAY & DAY - - *Dancing Time*

8. ITALO - - - - *Ace Juggler*

9. TOMMY FIELDS - - *More Laughs*

10. Here She Is!
The Famous Recording Star
WINIFRED ATWELL
Trinidad's Dynamic Queen of the Keys

11. JIMMY WHEELER - *Ay! Ay! That's Yer Lot*

12. ALL STAR ENSEMBLE

The Programmes

PROGRAMME

for week commencing MONDAY, 2nd AUGUST, 1954

1. OVERTURE - - *The Empire Orchestra*

2. REX & BESSIE - - - *Acro Dancers*

3. JOAN WINTERS & GUY FIELDING
   Radio's "Little Gal" and her Boy Friend

4. THREE HELLOS - *Continental Cyclists*

5. BENNY HILL
   Television's Funster Comedian
   with Jeremy Hawk

6. PEARL CARR
   Glamorous Singing Personality
   of Radio and Television

INTERMISSION
Selection - "TSCHAIKOWSKIANA" - arr. Palmer
THE EMPIRE ORCHESTRA
Under the direction of MAURICE NEWTON

FULLY LICENSED BARS IN ALL PARTS OF THE THEATRE
Favourite proprietary brands at Popular Prices
Whisky 2/-   Gin 1/9   Port and Sherry 2/-
Beers and Minerals at moderate prices

Programme continued overleaf

PROGRAMME
Continued

7. REX & BESSIE - *Dance Time Again*

8. JOAN WINTERS & GUY FIELDING
   Two Little Girls to Entertain You

9. REY OVERBURY
   The Musician with the Twinkling Feet
   Assisted by Suzette

10. BENNY HILL - - - *More Laughter*

11. TEDDY JOHNSON
    The Columbia Recording Star
    with Ernie Bragg at the Piano

PLEASE NOTE—PHOTOGRAPHING IN THE THEATRE IS FORBIDDEN

PROGRAMME

for week commencing MONDAY, 12th SEPTEMBER, 1955

1. OVERTURE - - *The Empire Orchestra*

2. SHANE & LAMAR - - - *Dance Time*

3. TWO NADIAS - *Juggling Cocktail*

4. KIRBY & HAYES - *Eccentric Funsters*

5. AUDREY JEANS - *Vivacious Comedy Star*

6. THE MARVELLOS
   American Novelty
   Music, Magic and Fun

7. CHIC MURRAY & MAIDIE
   New Comedy and Song

INTERMISSION
Selection - "BLUE SKIES" - Irving Berlin
THE EMPIRE ORCHESTRA
Under the direction of MAURICE NEWTON

FULLY LICENSED BARS IN ALL PARTS OF THE THEATRE

Programme continued overleaf

PROGRAMME
Continued

8. SHANE & LAMAR

9. TEX McLEOD - *Spinning Ropes and Yarns*

10. THE ANGELOS - - - *Aerialists*

11. CHIC MURRAY - *Here we are Again!*

12. Bernard Delfont presents
    The TV Radio and Recording Vocalist
    DAVID HUGHES
    At the Piano: Ronnie Loughhead

PLEASE NOTE—PHOTOGRAPHING IN THE THEATRE IS FORBIDDEN

The Programmes

PROGRAMME

Week commencing MONDAY, MARCH 31st, 1958
(INCLUDING GOOD FRIDAY)

1 OVERTURE ... The Empire Orchestra

2 NORMAN & NIKI GRANT Artistry in Rhythm

3 RAY ALAN ... ... Ventriloquist
and 'Steve'

4 THREE PAULOS ... ... Thrills in the Air

5 BILLY STUTT ... ... A Broth of a Boy

6 HEDLEY WARD TRIO
Vocal and Instrumental Group

INTERMISSION
Selection : "The King and I" ... Richard Rodgers
THE EMPIRE ORCHESTRA
Under the direction of MAURICE NEWTON

PROGRAMME CONTINUED OVERLEAF

FULLY LICENSED BARS IN ALL PARTS OF THE THEATRE

PROGRAMME
Continued

7 NORMAN & NIKI GRANT

8 RON & RITA ... Comedy on the Slack Wire

9 BILL WADDINGTON ... "Witty Willie"

10 ALMA COGAN
Glamorous Star of Stage, Radio and TV

The Management reserve the right to refuse admission to this theatre, and
to change, vary or omit, without previous notice, any item of the programme.

PLEASE NOTE—PHOTOGRAPHING IN THIS THEATRE IS FORBIDDEN

PROGRAMME
Continued

CARNIVAL ON ICE

OVERTURE .... The Empire Orchestra

1. "ROLL UP, ROLL UP!" .... The Circus Comes to Town
The Ringmaster .... Jan Tors
The Bareback Rider .... Jean Colquhoun
The Clown .... Reg. Moores
The Equestrian Trainer .... Luba Natova
The Liberty Horses .... The Ice Princesses
Clowns, Animals, etc., and the Entire Company

2. THE FOUR ESKIMOS .... The Abominable Ice Men
Bobby Brignell, Paul Stapleton, Martin Jakubait, Jimmy Peacock

3. "SAMBA, SAMBA" .... In Latin Manner
Jean Colquhoun, Dolores and Michael Arden, Pat Bowman and
The Ice Princesses

4. "CUBAN KATE" .... WONDROUS

5. DINKIE STAPLETON .... Acro-Ice-Trics

6. "AT THE ROYAL TOURNAMENT" .... The Musical Ride
The Ice Princesses

7. JAN TORS .... The Ace High Joker

8. "THE UNDERSEA BALLET" .... A Fantasy of the Ocean Depths
(a) Sea Anemones, (b) Starfish, (c) Coral, (d) Sea-Horses, (e) The
Sea Serpent. The Sea Wraith: Jean Colquhoun
The Pairs:
Luba Natova and Ron Stanley, Pat Bowman and Michael Arden,
Paddy Winter and Paul Stapleton, Gillian Sampson and Martin
Jakubait, and Ensemble with The Ice Princesses and Full Company

INTERMISSION
Selection - "WALTZING THRO' THE YEARS"
THE EMPIRE ORCHESTRA
Under the direction of MAURICE NEWTON

FULLY LICENSED BARS IN ALL PARTS OF THE THEATRE
Favourite proprietary brands at Popular Prices
Whisky 2/-   Gin 1/9   Port and Sherry 2/-
Beers and Minerals at moderate prices

Programme continued overleaf

PROGRAMME
Continued

9. "RHYTHM ON THE RINK" .... No Rough Edges
The Ice Princesses

10. REG. MOORES .... Stunts on Stilts

11. MARY and JIMMY SHERWOOD ...... Thrills and Spills for Laughs

12. LUBA NATOVA .... Skating for Your Delight

13. WONDROUS and MIMI .... Danse Apache

14. "THE BALLET OF THE ROSE" .... A Skating Dance Interpretation
Jean Colquhoun, Luba Natova, Pat Bowman, Martin Jakubait,
Paul Stapleton, Bobby Brignell, Michael Arden, and The Ice Princesses

15. "THE TERRIBLE TWINS" .... Presented by JAN TORS

16. WILLIAMS and SHAND .... Up High from Down Under

17. "SLOW and SOPHISTICATED" .... In Modern Manner
Luba Natova, Pat Bowman, Michael Arden, and The Ice Princesses

18. "THE CHARLADIES" .... Speeding Up the Cleaning Up
Bobby Brignell, Paul Stapleton, Martin Jakubait, Jimmy Peacock

19. JEAN COLQUHOUN .... A Dance Medley of Scotland

20. "THAT'S ALL FOR NOW" ..... The Entire Company make their
bows and hope you enjoyed the show
Goodnight, Good Luck, and Good Weather!

Music selected and arranged by Reginald Swinney
Scenery designed and painted by Edward Delany and constructed by Show Properties
Ltd. Costumes designed by Anthony Holland and executed by Dukes of Wardour Street
and Theatrical Models.

Production Manager	For	.... LOUIS BARBER
Musical Adviser	HOLIDAY ON ICE	.... REGINALD SWINNEY
Press Representative	(GREAT BRITAIN)	.... FRED GRATTON
Chief Refrigerating Engineer.....	LIMITED	...... O. M. MATTHEWS
Manager	For	.... RON HACKNEY
Musical Director...............	"CARNIVAL ON ICE"	...... LESTER HOSKIN
Ballet Mistress	COMPANY	.... JOSIE CORDREY

PLEASE NOTE—PHOTOGRAPHING IN THE THEATRE IS FORBIDDEN

28

The Programmes

PROGRAMME

for week commencing MONDAY, 30th JULY, 1956

1. OVERTURE - - *The Empire Orchestra*

2. THE THREE BALMORALS
   Ballet a la Can Can

3. LESLIE LESTER - - *The Debonair Deceiver*

4. MADRIGAL and Assistant
   International Uni-cyclist

5. BERT EDGAR - - *His Face is his Fortune*

6. FRED EMNEY - - - *If he's Arrived*

7. DIANA RHODES - - *A New Enterprise*

8. FRED EMNEY - - *If he Feels Like It*

INTERMISSION
THE EMPIRE ORCHESTRA
Under the direction of MAURICE NEWTON

FULLY LICENSED BARS IN ALL PARTS OF THE THEATRE

Programme continued overleaf

PROGRAMME
Continued

9. MONSIEUR DEFOE - - *Comical Shadows*

10. THE THREE BALMORALS
    A Breath of Heather

11. BETTY DRIVER - *The Dynamic Singing Star*
    with Wally Petersen
    At the Piano: Albert Sadler

12. FRED EMNEY - - *If he's Not in the Bar*

13. THE THREE BALMORALS
    Contrast in Rhythm

14. VIC SANDERSON - *Unique Australian Juggler*

The Management reserve the right to refuse admission to this theatre, and to change, vary, or omit, without previous notice, any item of the programme.

PLEASE NOTE—PHOTOGRAPHING IN THE THEATRE IS FORBIDDEN

OUR CHRISTMAS ATTRACTION

BOOK NOW FOR
EMILE LITTLER'S
Magnificent Pantomime
ALADDIN
NAT JACKLEY and JIMMY CLITHEROE
GREAT CAST OF PANTOMIME STARS

PROGRAMME

for week commencing MONDAY, JULY 27th, 1953

GASTON and ANDREE PRODUCTIONS present
ARTHUR LUCAN (Old Mother Riley) in

GOING GAY

A New Light-Hearted Frolic devised and produced by James Gaston and Rosemary Andree, with additional comedy sketches by Arthur Lucan.

Scene

1. "THE WEARING O' THE GREEN".... Full Company

2. "OLD MOTHER RILEY SAYS HELLO"
   ARTHUR LUCAN assisted by Ken Macey and Billy Mayne

3. "LADIES OF SPAIN"
   Singer .... SHEILA FRANCES
   Dancers .... THE FLORENCE WHITELEY GIRLS
   and Dot and Maureen

4. "GOOD NEIGHBOURS"
   OLD MOTHER RILEY .... ARTHUR LUCAN
   Ivy Ginnochie .... Gale Douglas
   Lancelot .... Malcolm Thomas

5. "UNDERNEATH THE ARCHES"
   Introducing Radio's Newest Singing Sensation
   THE STREET SINGERS

6. MACEY and MAYNE .... Just Crackers

7. "OLD MOTHER RILEY GOES WEST"
   Full Company (Acrobatic Speciality by Dot and Maureen)

INTERMISSION
Valse - STORIES OF THE VIENNA FOREST - Johann Strauss
THE EMPIRE ORCHESTRA
Under the direction of MAURICE NEWTON

FULLY LICENSED BARS IN ALL PARTS OF THE THEATRE
Favourite proprietary brands at Popular Prices
Whisky 2/- Gin 1/9 Port and Sherry 2/-
Beers and Minerals at moderate prices

Programme continued overleaf

PROGRAMME
Continued

Scene

8. "I LOVE A PARADE"
   Singer .... Sheila Frances
   Dancers .... THE FLORENCE WHITELEY GIRLS

9. "GETTING JOINED UP"
   OLD MOTHER RILEY .... ARTHUR LUCAN
   A Raw Recruit .... Gale Douglas
   Recruiting Officer .... Roy Rolland
   Medical Officer .... Ken Macey

10. "MUSICAL MEDLEY"
    Introducing CHARLES and JUPP
    Singer .... Sheila Frances
    Dancers .... THE FLORENCE WHITELEY GIRLS

11. THE STREET SINGERS
    In more songs you love to hear

12. "THE OLD MATCH SELLER"
    The Bride .... Gale Douglas

13. "AU REVOIR AGAIN" ....Full Company
    FINALE

Telephones by G.P.O.   Ladies' Stockings by Kayser Bondor

Manager and Stage Director .... C. WM. INGRAM
Stage Manager .... ELLIS ASHTON
Musical Director .... DIMITRI TSCHAKALOFF

The Management reserve the right to refuse admission to this theatre, and to change, vary, or omit, without previous notice, any item of the programme.

PLEASE NOTE—PHOTOGRAPHING IN THE THEATRE IS FORBIDDEN

The Programmes

PROGRAMME
for week commencing MONDAY, SEPT. 8th, 1952

1. OVERTURE - - *The Empire Orchestra*
2. REX & BESSIE - - - *- Acro Dancers*
3. RICHMAN & JACKSON - *The Lively Pair*
4. ESTRELLA SISTERS - - *Unusual Perchists*
5. SCOTT SANDERS - - *The Knife Grinder*
6. BILLY THORBURN - *Radio's Popular Pianist*

> **INTERMISSION**
> Selection - "THE GYPSY PRINCESS" - Kalman
> THE EMPIRE ORCHESTRA
> Under the direction of MAURICE NEWTON

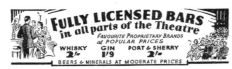

FULLY LICENSED BARS in all parts of the Theatre
Favourite Proprietary Brands at Popular Prices
WHISKY 2/- GIN 1/9 PORT & SHERRY 2/-
BEERS & MINERALS AT MODERATE PRICES

PROGRAMME
Continued

7. REX & BESSIE - - - *Entertain Again*
8. WALTER NIBLO - *Born Leeds—Sheffield thankful*
9.

The Queen of Glamour

GYPSY ROSE LEE

with her **AMERICAN BEAUTIES**

10. SCOTT SANDERS - - *The Old Actor*
11. PEPINO'S MINIATURE CIRCUS

PROGRAMME
for week commencing MONDAY, JULY 20th, 1953

TESSIE O'SHEA and JOHN FORBES-SEMPILL LTD.
present

TESSIE'S BIG SHOW

1. OVERTURE - - *The Empire Orchestra*
   "Tessie's in Town" .... *by Phil Park*
2. GRANDE FIESTA
   Dancers - - *The Granger Brothers*
   Singer - - - *Stuart Simpson*
   The Marie de Vere Lovelies
   and
   TESSIE O'SHEA
3. JOHNNY LOCKWOOD Introduces!
4. ST. DENIS BROS. & BERYL
   Acrobatically Different
5. MONA McCALL - *Singing Star from U.S.A.*
6. JOHNNY LOCKWOOD and DENNIS LAWES
   Prepare to go out for the Evening
7. JOHNNY MATSON - *American Entertainer*
8. The Marie de Vere Girls Introduce
   OLGA VARONA and her Aerial Ballet

> **INTERMISSION**
> Selection - "Jerome Kern Melodies" - arr. Henry Hall
> THE EMPIRE ORCHESTRA
> Under the direction of MAURICE NEWTON

FULLY LICENSED BARS IN ALL PARTS OF THE THEATRE
Favourite proprietary brands at Popular Prices
Whisky 2/- Gin 1/9 Port and Sherry 2/-
Beers and Minerals at moderate prices

Programme continued overleaf

PROGRAMME
Continued

9. "Just Painting the Clouds with Sunshine"
   Marie de Vere's
   Top o' the Town Lovelies
   introduce
   THE GRANGER BROTHERS
10. JOHNNY LOCKWOOD - *- Comedian*
11. "OUR" TESS
    Herself
    With Ernest Wampola at the Piano
    Leading to
    THE GRANGER BROTHERS
    The Marie De Vere Lovelies
    Miss Judy Garland????
    And the ENTIRE COMPANY
    in THE GRANDE FINALE

Costumes by R. St. John Roper, Lèonié Marié and Kritz of London

	For TESSIE O'SHEA	
Musical Director		.... JACK PUTNAM
Drummer	and	.... TOMMY JONES
Stage Director	JOHN FORBES-SEMPILL	.... DENNIS LAWES
Press Representative	LTD.	....PHILIP RIDGEWAY ASSC.

The Management reserve the right to refuse admission to this theatre, and to change, vary or omit, without previous notice, any item of the programme

PLEASE NOTE—PHOTOGRAPHING IN THE THEATRE IS FORBIDDEN

EMPIRE
SHEFFIELD

PROGRAMME THREEPENCE

The Programmes Covers

Variety

at the

EMPIRE
SHEFFIELD

PROGRAMME PRICE 3d.

VARIETY

AT THE

EMPIRE
SHEFFIELD

PROGRAMME PRICE THREEPENCE

The Programmes Covers

SHEFFIELD EMPIRE

PROGRAMME
PRICE THREEPENCE

The Programmes Covers

SHEFFIELD EMPIRE

PROGRAMME
PRICE THREEPENCE

The Programmes Covers

Tommy Steele appeared at the Sheffield Empire on 19/11/1956

Empire
THEATRE SHEFFIELD

chapter four

The Shows

Chapter Four
The Shows

As is shown within these listings, the Moss Empires provided a steady living for the many performers. Some of the star names were of course famous for their television appearances, films and/or recordings and consolidated this with their live appearances. For the other, lesser known names, the theatres were their only source of income and for them it would be an endless circle, travelling around the country, appearing at the different venues many times over. However they did enjoy their own measure of notoriety and popularity through their appearances whilst for other equally talented performers filling in variety bills was of course steady work, although they obviously enjoyed their careers in showbusiness.

The following listings are based purely on the information gathered together whilst researching for this book, CURTAIN UP AT THE EMPIRE, and are by no means complete.

1950

12th June

The very popular American singer **Allan Jones** starred in a variety show.

Also in **June** the star of radio's 'Variety Bandbox' **Reg 'Confidentially' Dixon** (*pictured right*) appeared together with **Margery Manners** along with supporting act **Allen Brothers & June**.

4th. September

"A Woman Desired" an adaptation of an original French show and strictly for adults. It starred a bevy of lovelies.

24th. December

Christmas Pantomime **'Humpty Dumpty'** starring comedian **Albert Modley with Ward Williams, Pamela Grant, Albert Grant** and full supporting cast.

1951

20th. August

"Showboat Express" was an all-male comedy revue and starred Britain's top female impersonators **Bartlett & Ross** and **Ford & Sheen**. Also in the cast as one of the 'Misleading Ladies', **Danny LaRue** was featured in his first speaking role.

1st October

A return of **Reg Dixon** in a show titled 'To Look At Me' and billed as a 'show of fun and spectacle'. Popular British crooner **Donald Peers** who had become famous for his song "By A Babbling Brook" also appeared.

26th November

Direct from London, Prince Littler's production of the Stage Musical **"Brigadoon"** played for three weeks.

3rd Decenber

Donald Peers (*autograph right*) returned to star in a variety show which included comedy duo **Morecambe & Wise** making an early Sheffield appearance, singer **Billy Danvers** and mad-cap novelty act **Dr. Crock & His Crackpots**.

1952

17th March

Starred popular radio/stage comedian **Al Read** with a show that included naughty comedienne **Iris Sadler** and ventriloquist **Arthur Worsley**.

31st May

30th June

The great American film comedy duo **Laurel & Hardy** headlined a special show for the week. Supporting acts included arial act **The Kenways**, **Saveen and Daisy May**, dance act **The Lonsdale Sisters**, singing cartoonist **Lorraine** and animal impressionist **Jimmie Elliot**.

Olly and Stan backstage at the Empire & (Autograph)

7th July

Starred the hugely popular Irish tenor **Josef Locke** Supporting act was the young comedy duo **Morecambe & Wise** (*pictured below*)

25th August

The popular **Ralph Reader's Gang Show** provide a full evening's entertainment . This would incorporate various mini stage plays and featuring an all-male cast of young actors and performers that Reader had selected from various boys' club in the UK. The second half of the evening's performance would see some of the performers featured in different routines of singing and dancing.

1st September

8th September

Rex and Bessie, Richman and Jackson, Estrella Sisters, Billy Thorburn, Scott Sanders, Walter Niblo, Gypsy Rose Lee, Pepino's Minature Circus.

29th September

Featured a mixed bill of musical performers **Geraldine & Joy**, comedy entertainers **Joy Jackley & Seth Jee**, acrobats **Trio Najarros**, ventriloquist act '**Daisy May**' with **Saveen**, musical comedy act **Hall, Norman & Ladd**. In the second half the programme would include the popular radio impressionist **Beryl Orde** with the top of the bill being the coloured American vocal group **The Deep River Boys**.

6th October

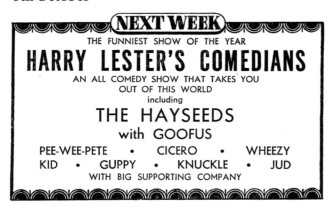

27th October

Saw the comedy showcase **'Open The Cage'** starring comedians **Arthur English** and 'Monsieur' **Eddie Gray**. Also on the bill were comedians **Donovan & Hayes**, trick cyclists **The Three Astons**, a mixture of singing and ballet from **Brian Kent**, **Maureen Rose** & **The Girls**. The second half also included musical comedy act **The Two Playboys**, **The Butlin American Square Dancers** ('The rage of the Country') with caller **Peggy Powell**. Another speciality on the bill were **The Viking Trio & Charmaine** with the **Eileen Rogan Girls**. Completing the show was **"Antimacassars & Old Laces"** (a dramatic episode of the year 1884)

3rd November

24th November

24th December

Christmas Pantomime **'Mother Goose'**, starring **Tommy Fields, Ruth Warner and Chevalier Brothers** with supporting cast.

1953

9th March

Flack & Lucas, Lester Sharpe & Iris, Louise with her Dogs & Ponies, George Doonan, The Radio Revellers, Del Cortina, The Lacey Troupe, popular songstress **Anne Shelton.**

16th March

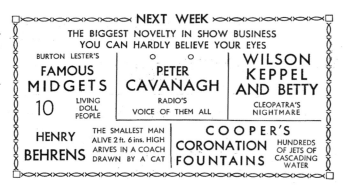

23rd March

NEXT WEEK
EVENINGS at 7.15
MATINEE: SATURDAY at 2.15

THE CROFT HOUSE SETTLEMENT OPERATIC SOCIETY
present

THE DANCING YEARS
(By arrangement with Tom Arnold Ltd.)
DEVISED, WRITTEN and COMPOSED by
IVOR NOVELLO

30th March

Featured a variety bill under the heading *"Your Song Parade"* with Marie De Vere's **Cover Girls** dance troupe, comedienne **Hylda Baker,** balancing act **The Five Furres**, comedy magic from **Gaston Palmer** and canine comedians **Darly's Dogs** The second half opened to the beat of Rhumba Time with Marie De Vere's **Cover Girls** again then a sketch titled 'Girls In he Home Guard' featuring **Hylda Baker** and friend followed by more from Marie De Vere's **Cover Girls** before ventriloquist **Arthur Worsley** and then **Lester Ferguson** who invited everybody to a family circle of song.

April 6th

Star attraction was the popular singing/whistler **Ronnie Ronalde**

13th April

Norman and Nikki Grant, Phil Darban and Wendy, Fred Lovelle, Lizzet and Eddie, Lionel King, Allen and Lee, Bobby Black, Eddie Gordon, comedian **Al Read**

20th April

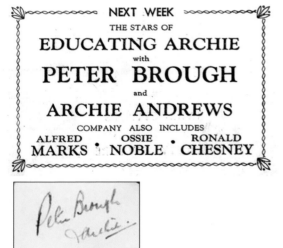

NEXT WEEK
THE STARS OF
EDUCATING ARCHIE
with
PETER BROUGH
and
ARCHIE ANDREWS
COMPANY ALSO INCLUDES
ALFRED · OSSIE · RONALD
MARKS · NOBLE · CHESNEY

April 27th

A production of **"Pull Up At Dave's"** written and produced by the 'Big Head' **Dave Morris** made up the week's bill. This was a series of short stage-plays which starred **Morris** along with his cast of actors and actresses who included northern character actor **Joe Gladwin**. The first half featured three sketches; *'Outside The Television Studio', 'Scandal Outside The Co-op'* and *'Behind The Iron Curtain'*. Balancing act **The Three Rethlems, The**

Balcombes – fun on a revolving ladder and vocalist **Bette Lee**, dancers **The Glamorettes**, tap-dancers **Christine & Moll**, musical group from Australia **The Dargie Quintet** and more from **The Glamourettes**.

From May 1953 the Empire Programmes would feature a regal colour picture of Her Majesty on the front cover showing her entering The London Palladium. The occasion was on November 3rd when she honoured the Variety Profession with her presence at a performance of The Variety Artistes' Benevolent Fund. This was also in Her Majesty The Queen's Coronation Year.

The Sheffield Empire Programme   Price threepence

May 4th

Special all-laughter variety show starring **Norman Evans** with **Betty Jummel** co-starring.

11th May

'Rockin' In Rhythm' with **Conway and Day, George Meaton, Ted and George Durante,** comedians **Joe Church, Jimmy Wheeler, Tommy Fields, Italo,** and star pianist and recording artist **Winifred Atwell.**

18th May

22nd June

25th May

Following opening comedy act **Vi, Joe & Vic Havard** this night was given over to an evening of **Carroll Levis Discoveries.** which included a selection of his latest Radio and television discoveries. **Levis** would present the show along with *'Glamorous Young TV, Radio & Screen Star'* **Violet Pretty** along with a selection of Teenage performers. After the interval Levis reappeared to bring on his latest discoveries from his TV and radio shows. These included Sheffield's Personality Girl **Margaret Harrison** and Sheffield's own boy accordionist **Toni Abbott**.

29th June

1st June

6th July

8th June

Comedy show **Fred Karno's Army** featuring the **Four Graham Brothers, Eleanor Cam's Can-Can Ma'm-selles, Bertie Sellers, Irene Dickson, Peggy French.**

15th. June

Merle and Marie, Peter Raynor, Will Carr and Partner, Bob Andrews, 'Britain's Street Singer' **Gwen Liddle, Don Phillipe and Marta, Raydini, Ray Overbury** assisted by **Suzette, The Merry Macs.**

20th July

Tessie's Big Show', starring **Tessie O'Shea,** *(pictured right)* **Johnny Lockwood, St. Denis Bros and Beryl, Mona McCall, Johnny Matson, Olga Varona, The Granger Brothers.**

27rd July

Show titled **'Going Gay'** and starring **Arthur Lucan** as **Old Mother Riley** with full supporting company.

3rd August

NEXT WEEK
ARCHIE PARNELL & COMPANY present
A NEW SPECTACULAR COMEDY REVUE
CHOCOLATE & CREAM
BEING A FAREWELL VISIT TO SHEFFIELD
OF
G. H. ELLIOTT The Chocolate
Coloured Coon
JACK TRIPP—New Revue Comedian
and GUEST ARTISTE
LESLIE WELSH—The Memory Man

10th August

'Anna Lucasta', an American play.

17th August

'French Mustard' Comedy Revue featuring '**Ossie Morris, Tommy Jover and Company, Raf and Julian,** 'Floral Rhythm' **Three Burgess Brothers,** 'Double Event' 'As Bold As Brass', **Dumarte and Denzar.**

August 24th

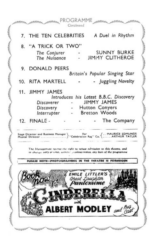

August 31st

Headlining this was show was the popular American recording star **Rose Murphy** with support from impressionist **Clifford Stanton, Beryl and Bobo, Rex and Bessie, Walthon and Dorraine, Ron Parry, The Osmani Troupe, Freddie Harris & Betty.**

7th September

NEXT WEEK
AMERICA'S FAMOUS COLOURED HARMONY TEAM
FREDDIE BAMBERGER and PAM
"Jest Artistes"
THE DEEP RIVER BOYS
HALL, NORMAN & LADD Musical Zombies
AND BIG SUPPORTING COMPANY

14th September

Starred another major singing star of he 50's **David Whitfield, Renee Strange, Hal Monty, Paula Coutts, Tommy Dale, Two Sterlings, Andree Jan.**

21st September

Featured the singing troupe, **The Five Smith Brothers** (Roy, Harold, Stan, Alf and Ronnie) in a special show titled 'The Smiths Come To Town'. Following the Overture the Company sang "How do you do" to Sheffield. The little lady from China **Delly Kin**, comic **Roy Smith**, mad musician **Billy Crotchet**, grace and acrobats **Five Jays & A June**, crazy funsters **Syd & Max Harrison** and closing the first half with 'Fifty Years Of Song' This would feature the company in a selection of vintage popular songs.

5th October

For a run of two weeks **Roy Barbour** would star the touring London production of **"Zip Goes A Million"** – 'The Zippiest, Snappiest and Happiest Musical In Town' and featuring the full company from the Palace Theatre, London.

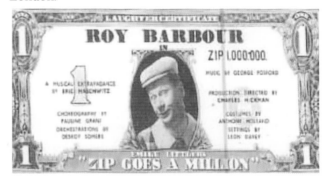

12th. October

NEXT WEEK
6.15 TWICE NIGHTLY 8.30
THOSE GREAT FUNSTERS
JIMMY JEWEL AND **BEN WARRISS**
with BIG CAST
IN THEIR NEW COMEDY SHOW
KEEP 'EM LAUGHING

19th October

'Pull Up At Dave's' starring **Dave Morris and Company**, **Arabell and Carlson**, **Bette Lee**, **Carren and Coostal**, **The Glamourettes**, **The Dargie Quintet**.

26th October

Starting with dancers **Norman & Niki Grant**, and continuing with comedian **Joe Black**, roller-skating balancing act **The Columbus**, Radio sporting impressionist **Tony Fayne & David Evans** and glamour dance-troupe **Dawn White** and her **Glamazons** singing cartoonist **Lorraine**, uni-cyclists **The Western Stars**, comedy actor **Bernard Miles** and headliner the popular singing star **Frankie Vaughan**.

2nd November

Coinciding with Sheffield Rag Week the Sheffield University Students Union staged a special fund-raising **"Rag Revue 1953"** and featuring guest artist **'Cheerful' Charlie Chester** plus an all-student cast.

16th November

Presented another variety programme with Radio, TV and film star **Reg 'Confidentially' Dixon** topping the bill. Support came Sword Dancers **The Balmorals**, female comedy act **Fe Jover**, saucy comedienne **Iris Sadler**, **Vera Cody** and her horse **'Goldie'**, ventriloquist **Terry Hall**, musical comedy act **Don Saunders**. The second half saw **The Balmorals** and **Iris Sadler** going through their paces once again before the film star dogs **'Gorin' & 'Domino'** also presented by **Vera Cody**.

23rd November

With a run of three weeks The Empire played host to Tom Arnold's spectacular production of the musical **"Chu Chin Chow"** on Ice.

7th December

'Top Of The Town's Talent' with **Carroll Levis** Sheffield talent versus talent from Surrounding Sheffield

24th December

Christmas Panto, **'Cinderella'** with **Albert Modley**

29th March

April 5th

19th April

Conway and Day, **Freddie Harrison**, **Three Lesters**, musical novelty act **Albert & Les Ward**, comedian **Tommy Fields**, **Alex and Nico**, **Rob Murray**, popular recording stars **The Beverley Sisters**.

26th April

Zany comedian **Max Wall**, comedian/singer **Alfred Marks**, **Joan Mann**, comedian **Freddie Frinton** with **Sonnie Willis**, **Max and Harry Nesbitt**, **Seaton and O'Dell**, **The Skating Sayers** and **'Professor Walofski'**

3rd May

The Vocalettes and Vernon Sisters, **Syd Seymour**, **'Chicken Reel'**, **El Granadas and Peter**, **Ernest Arnley and Gloria Day**, **Donald B. Stuart**, musical comedy act **The Maestro and his Seemfunny Orchestra**, **A Night At The Empire (Cast)**.

10th May

NEXT WEEK
TESSIE O'SHEA
"TWO TONS OF FUN"
and introducing Pianist and Composer
ERNEST WAMPOLA
and
THE DON HUNTER SWING QUINTET

TOMMY JOVER AND COMPANY	ARTHUR WORSLEY	MUNDY & EARLE
	PLUS BIG COMPANY	

17th May

Rey and Ronjy, Sally and Charles, comedy star **Terry Scott,** pianist supreme **Semprini, Jon Pertwee, Joyce Golding, Paul and Peta Page** and comedy vocal group **The Radio Revellers.**

24th May

NEXT WEEK
WILL COLLINS presents
RHYTHM IS THEIR BUSINESS
with
BRITAIN'S TOP VOCALIST
LITA ROZA

JIMMY JAMES and COMPANY	WILSON, KEPPEL & BETTY
DARGIE QUINTET AUSTRALIAN RHYTHM ENSEMBLE	PLUS BIG BILL

31st May

'Knights Of Madness' with comedian **Eddie Gray, Willie Carlisle,** comedy character **Arthur English** and **Dave and Joe O'Gorman.**

7th June

American singing and recording star **Al Martino**

FOR ONE WEEK ONLY
AMERICA'S EXCITING
NEW VOICE
AL MARTINO
Brilliant Recorder of
"Here in my Heart" · "Rachel"
"Now" · "Take My Heart"
"I Never Cared"
WITH BIG SUPPORTING COMPANY

14th June

The Knife-Throwing Denvers, Joan and Ernest, The Original Garcas, Reggie Dennis, unique pianist **Tom Jacobson, The Motor-Cycling Mikowskis, Ladd West, The Four Kelroys,** escapologist **Alan Alan.**

21st June

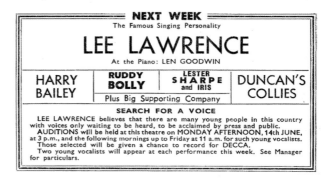

NEXT WEEK
The Famous Singing Personality
LEE LAWRENCE
At the Piano: LEN GOODWIN

HARRY BAILEY	RUDDY BOLLY	LESTER SHARPE and IRIS	DUNCAN'S COLLIES
	Plus Big Supporting Company		

SEARCH FOR A VOICE
LEE LAWRENCE believes that there are many young people in this country with voices only waiting to be heard, to be acclaimed by press and public. AUDITIONS will be held at this theatre on MONDAY AFTERNOON, 14th JUNE, at 3 p.m., and the following mornings up to Friday at 11 a.m. for such young vocalists. Those selected will be given a chance to record for DECCA. Two young vocalists will appear at each performance this week. See Manager for particulars.

28th June

A mixed bag opening with leggy dancers **The Four Glamourettes** before '*Mummy Do It First*' a comedy sketch featuring **Ken Morris, Mimi Law** and **Billy Whittaker** with **Wally Peterson.** Singing act The Shipway Twins, musical entertainers **Ken Morris** with **Joan Savage.** Mime act **Authors & Swinson,** acrobatic xylophonist **Tommy Dale** then comedy actor **Leslie Randall** and then bubbly Radio and TV singing star **Betty Driver** topping the bill.

5th July

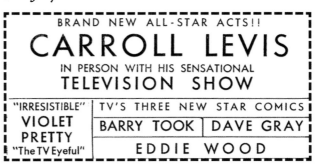

BRAND NEW ALL-STAR ACTS!!
CARROLL LEVIS
IN PERSON WITH HIS SENSATIONAL
TELEVISION SHOW

"IRRESISTIBLE" VIOLET PRETTY "The TV Eyeful"	TV'S THREE NEW STAR COMICS	
	BARRY TOOK	DAVE GRAY
	EDDIE WOOD	

12th July

Another variety bill starting with dancing lovelies **The Six Roy Belles,** then comedian **Bill Waddington,** glamourous acrobatic act **Frances Duncan,** star TV impressionist **Peter Cavanagh,** popular singing starlet **Julie Dawn,** star pianist and arranger **Bill McGuffie,** topical comedian **Albert Sturm** and a display of whip and ropes **Rex Roper & Pat**.

19th July

```
┌ ─ ─ ─ ─ ─ ─ ─ ─ ─ ─ ─ ─ ─ ─ ─ ─ ┐
   COLUMBIA'S SENSATIONAL RECORDING STAR
│  TONY  BRENT                      │

│  MORTON  FRASER'S                 │
   HARMONICA  GANG
│ ───────────────────────────────  │
   GEORGE  &  ANNE  DOONAN
│ ───────────────────────────────  │
   HILLBILLY  POLECATS
│     AND  FULL  COMPANY            │
└ ─ ─ ─ ─ ─ ─ ─ ─ ─ ─ ─ ─ ─ ─ ─ ─ ┘
```

26th July

Customary dancing openers **Kim & Pam Lewington**, musical act **Hackford & Doyle**, acrobat **Jolly**, slapstick comedians **Bobby Wright & Marion**, singer guitarist **Malcolm Mitchell** and his **Men Of Music**. Dance duo **Kim & Pam Lewington** popular female singing star of radio, TV and records **Alma Cogan,** comedy actor **Michael Bentine** with acrobatic team **The Three Henrys**.

2nd August

Acrobatic-dancers **Rex & Bessie**, Radio's "Little Gal" **Joan Winters** and her boyfriend **Guy Fielding**, continental cyclists **Three Hellos**, television comedian **Benny Hill** accompanied by straight man **Jeremy Hawk** with perky songstress **Pearl Carr** musician/dancer **Rey Overbury** assisted by **Suzette**. Columbia Records singing star **Teddy Johnson** ended the night.

9th August

```
┌ ─ ─ ─ ─ ─ ─ ─ ─ ─ ─ ─ ─ ─ ─ ─ ─ ┐
│     PETE  COLLINS'                │
        GIANT
│  SPACE  SHIP                      │

│ A TRIP TO THE MOON WITHOUT LEAVING YOUR SEAT! │
   ───────────────────────────────
│  Actual journey through Space—from Blast-Off to Landing │
    seen on the Space Ships' Giant Televisor!
└ ─ ─ ─ ─ ─ ─ ─ ─ ─ ─ ─ ─ ─ ─ ─ ─ ┘
```

16th August

Saw a week of musical drama with the World Famous Melodrama *"East Lynne"* presented by **Mr. Hubert Wood**

23rd August

Popular singing star **Dickie Valentine** starred with **Nenette Mongadors and Ann, Jackson, Bow and Darnel, Richman and Jackson, Joe Church, Eddie Gordon, Susie, Charles Warren and Jean.**

30th August

More variety with dancers **The Roybelles**, novelty act **The Ken Dorvilles**, return of saucy comedienne **Iris Sadler**, arial act **The Skylons** and the golden-voiced comedian from the Goon Show and 'Educating Archie' **Harry Secombe**, topping the bill were musical comedy ensemble **Dr. Crock And His Crackpots**.

6th September

"Carnival On Ice" featuring *'Glamour!, Spectacle! Comedy!* And featuring a *'fine cast of skating personalities'.* **The Four Eskimos, 'Samba Samba', 'Cuban Kate', Dinkie Stapleton, The Under Sea Ballet, Jan Tors, Reg Moores, May and Jimmy Sherwood, Luba Natova, Wondrous and Mimi. Jean Colquhoun, The Charladies.**

13th September

```
┌ ─ ─ ─ ─ ─ ─ ─ ─ ─ ─ ─ ─ ─ ─ ─ ─ ┐
│ STARS OF THE SHOW BAND SHOW      │

│ Two Crazy │ The B.B.C.'s │ Introducing │ Cavalcade │
   Funsters                            of Humour
│ SYD       │ RAY      │          │ BILLY     │
   and        BURNS      BILL
│ MAX       │          │ McGUFFIE │ BAXTER    │
   HARRISON   Columbia
│ "Just Nuts" │ Recording │ Ace Pianist │ Plus Big Bill │
              Star
└ ─ ─ ─ ─ ─ ─ ─ ─ ─ ─ ─ ─ ─ ─ ─ ─ ┘
```

4th October

Presented the farewell tour of **The Quaker Girl** the spectacular musical produced by **Emile Littler**.

11th October

Commenced with dance team **Mills & Melita**, sketch artist **Peggy Cavell**, animal act **Louise** with her **Dogs & Pony**, comedy magicians **Jay Palmer & Doreen**, zany comedian/musician **Stan Stennett**, ventriloquist **Austral**, singing and recording star **Joan Regan** then star comedian **Jimmy Wheeler** daredevil fetes from high wire act **Del Cortina**.

18th October

BERNARD DELFONT presents

THE WORLD FAMOUS

RAY ELLINGTON QUARTET with **MARION RYAN**

Hear them in B.B.C's Goon Show, "Mr. Ros and Mr. Ray" Series and on Parlophone, Decca and Columbia Records

Star Comedians of Radio and T.V. Fame

MORECAMBE AND WISE "YOU'RE ONLY YOUNG ONCE"

With Full Variety Company

Philips' Sensational Recording Star **GARY MILLER**

1st November

Featured *'The Trinder Show'* which starred the popular comedian/actor **Tommy Trinder** accompanied by the **George Mitchell Quartet** and **The Larry Gordon Girls**. The supporting show consisted of high flying act **The Six Flying De Pauls**, vocalist **Pat Galloway**, duo **Woods & Jarrett**. puppet act **Salici Puppets**, trick cyclists **Two Arvings**, *'A Chinese Drama'* featuring **Harry Moreny**, another comedy feature *'Not As Bad As We're Painted'* featuring **Ann Hart and The Girls** with **Trinder** himself completing the show.

8th November

Originally it should have been the famous Irish tenor **Joseph Locke** starring but for some reason he did not appear and instead the programme was another mixed bill with dancers **The Lee Youngsters**, radio's husky comic **Billy Maxman**, versatile performers **Margo Henderson & Sam Kemp**, amusing manipulator **Rolph Hansen** and **Alexander's Dog Revue**. **The Lee Youngsters**, novelty acrobats **The Marettas**, popular singing star **Cavan O'Connor**, comedian **Joe King** and youthful musical group **Larry Macari Quintet**.

THE IRISH TENOR

JOSEF LOCKE

— with —

FULL SUPPORTING VARIETY COMPANY

15th November

A Special production of Rodgers & Hammerstein's ever-popular **"South Pacific"** starring **Patricia Hartley** and **Nevil Whiting**

13th December

Featured more variety with staircase dancer **Bunty St.Clair**, comedy performer **Bruce Forsyth**, Arial act **The Rosinas**, silent humorist **Eddie Vitch**, vintage singing duo **Bob & Alf Pearson**. **Don Philippe & Marta** 'design to delight', working-class comedian **Billy Russell** and once again, c/o Bernard Delfont, the popular recording, TV and film star **Frankie Vaughan** and accompanied by his regular pianist **Bert Waller.**

20th December

Christmas Panto of **'Aladdin'** with **Nat Jackley** and **Jimmy Clitheroe** starring.

1955

18th April

Television comedy performer **Max Wall** with customary opening dancing act **Marie De Vere Trio**, comedian **Peter Dulay**, dynamic spark **Joan Mann**, and then **Max Wall** did his first spot. Finishing off the first half was **The Sorcerer and his Apprentices** featuring **Benson Dulay & Company**. International dancers **Marie De Vere Trio** came back on to open the second half followed by a presentation of *'Honeysuckle'* with **Claudine** with **Trevor Hill**, ventriloquist **Terry Hall** with **'Mickey Flynn'** and **'Lenny The Lion'** and vocal group **The Kentones**. The show then finished off with **Max Wall** again, this time in the guise of **"Professor Walloffski"**

25th April

Here Monday, 25th April

FOR TWO WEEKS

Bernard Delfont presents

(by arrangement with M. PAUL DERVAL and MICHEL GYARMATHY)

The REAL FRENCH SHOW from PARIS

VIC OLIVER

and GIGANTIC CAST IN THE NEW SENSATIONAL

FOLIES BERGERE REVUE

PARDON MY FRENCH

Produced by DICK HURRAN

16th May

'Women Of Twilight'

23rd. May

London promoter **Stanley Dale** presented a special variety bill in which was hosted by **Sally Rogers** with Arial act **The Two Aeros**, comedian **Frankie Howerd**, high-wire act **Brian Andro**, TV ventriloquist **Bobby Kimber**, comedy star **Bobby Page**, musical comedy **'Serenade In Spain'** featuring **Kenneth Birrell** as Don Carlos, **Sally Rogers** as Senorita Alvalro and **Frankie Howerd** as Senor Francisco. Billed as Britain's New Vocal Stylist was **Lee Young**. continental comedy acrobats **The Vadios Bros.**, illusionist **The Great Fredini**, girl trumpeter **Joan Hinde**, female juggler **Rita Martell**, **Frankie Howerd**, assisted by **Madam Blanchie Moore** at the piano *"poor soul"*

30th May

6th June

Averil and Aurel, Freddie Harrison The Three Kelroys, Jack Storey, Nino, Fred Lovelle, Joan and Ernest, hit recording star **Ronnie Hilton**

June 13th

Opened with the unusual girl **Renee Dymott** continuing with ventriloquist **Dick Calkin**, **Derrick Rosaire** presented his Wonder Horse **'Tony'**, **Gaston Palmer** had 'all the spoons in the glasses' followed by popular singing four-piece **The Radio Revellers** to wind up the first half. After the interval **Renee Dymott** danced again before dog-act **Betty Kaye's Pekinese Pets** followed by joker **Lionel King** and finished with popular singing star on television and records **Anne Shelton**.

27th June

'Guys And Dolls', 'direct from 555 performances at the London Coliseum'.

4th. July

25th July

Gale and Clark, Cyril Dowler and **Rhoda Rogers**, **Marion and Eddie Rose**, comedian **Archie Glen**, organist & singer **Cherry Wainer**, **Alan Kemble and Christine**, popular singer **Josef Locke**

1st August

8th August

August 22nd

The McKinnon Sisters followed by balancing act **Maurice French** and partner, comedy act **Cecil Sheridan**. A second balancing act were the **Duo Russmar** continuing with singing comedian **Tommy Fields**, radio and recording star **Diana Decker**. TV's new star comedian **Jimmy Edmundson**. Puppetry with **Buckmaster's Puppets** with the *Original 'Jones Boy'* **Reggie Arnold**

August 29th

THE RADIO AND TV COMEDIAN BAND
SID MILLWARD - WALLY STEWART
and the
NITWITS
Music ? in the Millward Manner
MANLEY & AUSTIN
Music Hath Charms

The Popular Dame Comedian
GEORGE LACY
"She's No Lady"
NANETTE MONGADORS and ANNE

Ambassadors of Song
THE RAMBLERS
COOPER TWINS

5th September

Jackson, Bow and Darnel, Richman and Jackson, Joan and Jack Wins, comedy magician **Albert Burden & Co., Harriot and Evans, Mandy and Sandy, Dargie Quintet,** popular vocalist **Tony Brent.**

12th September

Shane & Lamar followed by jugglers **Two Nadias,** eccentric funsters **Kirby & Hayes, Audrey Jeans** act **The Marvellos** comedian **Chic Murray** and his assistant **Maidie.** cowboy act **Tex McLeod,** Arial act **The Angelos,** popular TV and recording star of the day, **David Hughes.**

19th September

A special presentation by the well known Soho impresario **Paul Raymond** titled **"Las Vegas"** and billed as *'The Fabulous American Show in the wonder of Stereophonic Sound'* the show also boasted that it also *'plunges you with a startling new ultra modern era of stage entertainment'.* Featuring **Desmond Lane, Fran Dowdie** and **Sandi Kane, Jack Anton.**

3rd. October

EVENINGS at 7.15   WED. & SAT. 2 performances at 5.0 & 8.0

GEORGE & ALFRED BLACK present
EVELYN LAYE
BARRY SINCLAIR
in the Romantic Musical Comedy
WEDDING IN PARIS
The Entire West End Production Direct from the London Hippodrome

17th October

Another variety bill with the versatile **Clarkson & Leslie,** singing duo **Shipway Twins,** comedy jugglers Harry Allen with **The Albee Sisters,** canine act **Darley's Dogs,** northern comedian **Joe Crosbie** and a riot of fun and music from **The Musical Elliots.** ventriloquist **Saveen** with and **'Daisy May'** and dynamic US singing group **The Deep River Boys.**

24th October

Kicked off with dance team **Bea & Zelda Marvi** followed by whirlwind tumbling from **The Mantanzas,** comedy duo **Raf & Julian Jover, Albert Modley** playing the part of a young lad in a comedy sketch titled "Albert Joins The Cubs" with **Lynda Ross** as his Mother and **Bert Lindon** as his Father. Concluding the first half was the glamorous singing star **Pearl Carr.** Western performer **Sunny Rogers** recording star **Teddy Johnson** closing the show.

31st October

Promoters **Gaston & Andree** presented *'A Real French Revue',* **"The French Peep Show"** starring **Jimmy Gay** and **Iris Poliakova** *'Europe's beautiful model'.*

7th November

14th November

EVENINGS at 7.15   WED. & SAT. 2 Performances at 5.0 & 8.0
GEORGE FORMBY
in
A PRIOR TO LONDON LAUGHTER SHOW
Emile Littler's
"TOO YOUNG TO MARRY"

21st November

'Ladies For Hire' stage-play

28th November

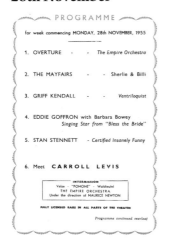 

5th. December

THE FUNNIEST SHOW OF THE YEAR!
HARRY LESTER'S COMEDIANS
IN AN ALL COMEDY-THRILL SHOW
with his
HAYSEEDS
in Hilarious Haywire Harmony

1956

27th February

The House Of Shame a stage play.

5th March

Ivor Novello's musical **The King's Rhapsody** staged by **The Croft House Operatic Society**

16th April

'Call Girl' stage drama including cast members **Robert Vaughan** and **Arthur White**

23rd April

More variety with opening dancers **Anton & Janetta** then arialist **Anita** followed by return of comedy duo **Hackford & Doyle**, comedy jugglers **Harry Allen** and **The Albee Sisters**, comedian **Hal Garner** and acrobatoic novelty act **Les Marthys,** the popular singing and recording star **Dickie Valentine**.

30th. April

HYLDA BAKER
"SHE KNOWS Y'KNOW!"
with
FULL SUPPORTING COMPANY

7th May

Rey and Ronjy, **Pat Rosa, Bobby Wright and Marion, Lizzet and Eddie, Roger Carne** with 'Canasta', 'Wonder Bar' featuring **Milton Woodward, The Morlands, Ron Parry** and American singing star **Don Cornell**.

14th May

 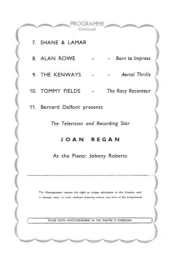

21st May

Opening act was **Kay & Kimberley** followed by the **Skating Meteors**, TV's 'newsboy' **Billy Maxam**, the acrobatic **Felixio**, laughter duo **Syd & Paul Kaye** and organist/singer **Cherry Wainer, The Buckmaster Puppets**, topping the bill, 'King of the Discs' **Jimmy Young**.

28th May

Presenting 'a new exciting continental style revue' **La Revue Des Filles** (The Revue Of Girls) and starring **Johnny Lockwood** with full supporting company.

4th June

Paul Raymond's Vanities of 1956 with '**Paris After Dark**', **Tommy Godfrey, The Lyndons**.

11th June

Britain's Foremost Comedienne **GLADYS MORGAN** with her Laugh and company	Radio's Brilliant Impressionist **PETER CAVANAGH** The Voice of them all	**CHIC MURRAY** and **MAIDIE** In a New Comedy offering	**LEE YOUNG** New Vocal Stylist
	With full Supporting Company		

25th June

Roy Smith, Freddie Harrison, Jimmy Paige, Betty Fox, Buster Fiddess, The Brazillianos, Les Mallini, Arthur Tolchar, vocal team **The Five Smith Brothers.**

2nd July

Sydney Productions Ltd. present
THE STAR-DUST SHOW
UNE NUIT D'AMOUR
"ONE NIGHT OF LOVE"
SYD SEYMOUR
AND HIS MADHATTERS
with
BILLY REVEL and PAT FIELDS · CONSTANCE EVANS · TREBLE TONES
NUDES DE DESIRE AND LES BALLET DE PARIS

9th. July

'French Follies Revue' with comedian **Jimmy Gay, The Ladringlos, The French Can-Can Dancers,** LeWhite And His Gal, Fan-dancer **Iris Poliakova, Jack Whiteley's Folies Girls, Ron Dillon, Eddie and Jac Romano** and vocal duo, the **Prince Sisters.**

16th. July

HINGES PRODUCTIONS LTD. PRESENT
THE MERRY MAGPIES
The Happy-Go-Lucky Family Entertainment
BOBBY THOMPSON
Durham's Own Radio Star of "Bob's Your Uncle"
MICHAEL HIBBERT
The North's Greatest Tenor
GENE PATTON
AND BIG SUPPORTING COMPANY

23rd July

Variety bill with high-wire act **Georgette** opening followed by new style comedian **Ron Scott,** dynamic dance team **The Granger Brothers,** actor/comedian **Cardew Robinson** and contortionist **Eleanor Gunter,** harmonica hotshots **Hill & Billy,** comedy illusionists **Lester Sharpe & Iris** and finishing off, recording star **Lee Lawrence.**

30th July

The Three Balmorals opened up with ballet a la Can-Can, illusionist **Leslie Lester,** uni-cyclists **Madrigal** and Assistant. Actor Bert, *'Outsize'* TV and film personality **Fred Emney,** new starlet **Diana Rhodes,** comical shadows of **Monsieur Defoe.** vivacious singing star **Betty Driver** unique Australian juggler **Vic Sanderson** closing the bill.

6thAugust

Featured **The Mayfairs** dance team, ventriloquist **Fred Atkins,** international jugglers **The Carals,** vocal outfit **Group One** from Radio's 'Back With Braden', British Heavyweight champion of humour **Max Bacon,** 'Memory Man' **Leslie Welch,** Radio & TV stars **Nat Mills with Mitzi** and finishing off with new singing sensation **Ronnie Carroll**

13th August

DIRECT FROM AMERICA
VIRGIL
The Premier International Illusionist
World Famous Musical Revue
MAGICANA
25 Breathtaking Scenes
Featuring
JULIE
The Sweetheart of Magic with
16 Dazzling Glamour Girls

20th August

'Showboat Express' an all male camp comedy revue with a cast of international female impersonators featuring **Bartless & Ross, Ford & Sheen, Douglas Harris, Les Morgan,** accordianists **Les Flores,** Bruce Calder, Douglas Curries, **Pierre Zampa** and his **'Ondioline', Les Dounos, Bennie Humphries** and the **Express Lovelies.**

1st October

Variety show starring songstress **Dorothy Squires** with dance team **The Edorics**, ventriloquist **Jack Beckett**, Comedy magic routine with **Albert Burden**, **The Singing Songsters**, music and fun with **The Musical Elliots**, thrills and spills with **Bernie and Maggie Harris**.

8th October

The 'King Of Skiffle' **Lonnie Donegan** with **Mundy and Early**, musical comedy star **Stan Stennet, Marie De Vere Dancers**, young comedian **Des O'Connor**, **Curzon Trio, Griff Kendall, Mike McKenzie**.

15th October

'Rock'n'Roll Show' with Tony Crombie and his **Rockets**, singers **Maxine Daniels, Don Fox, Bill Wyner**.

22nd October

From The Drury Lane, the production of Rodgers' & Hammerstein's **"The King & I"**.

5th November

Opening with **Ann & Val Shelley** dance team, continuing with comics **Vic Gordon & Peter Colville**, arialist **The Angelos**, comedy impressionist **Jackie Ross** an glamorous singing stars **The Tanner Sisters**. Part two had the second stints by **Ann & Val Shelley** and **Vic Gordon & Peter Colville**. Popular singing star **Michael Holiday** preceded comedy star **Ken Platt** with trampoline act **Kazan & Katz** closing.

12th November

CARROLL LEVIS
presenting the Latest and Greatest
TELEVISION CHAMPIONS
THE DISCOVERIES OF TODAY
ARE THE STARS OF TOMORROW
—— PLUS ——
FULL VARIETY COMPANY

19th November

Britain's top rock'n'roll star **Tommy Steele & His Steelmen** heading a show along with comedians **Mike & Bernie Winters, Marie DeVere Dancers**, comedian **Reg Thompson**, crazy music with the one man band **Johnny Laycock**, keyboard wizard **Thunderclap Jones** and **Josephine Ann** from the Crazy Gang.

FIRST LONDON THEATRE APPEARANCE!
ROCK WITH TOMMY STEELE
DECCA'S DYNAMIC RECORDING STAR singing his best sellers — " Rock with the Caveman ", " Doomsday Rock " and " Singing the Blues ".
Presented by HAROLD FIELDING
ALL NEXT WEEK! SHEFFIELD EMPIRE
Twice Nightly at 6.25 & 8.40 p.m.
"He's Great, Great, Great ".
—Ker Robertson, 'Daily Sketch'

26th November

Eddie Calvert Productions Ltd.
present
"CALVERT CAVALCADE"
starring
The Man with the Golden Trumpet
EDDIE CALVERT
GERRY BRERETON
BILLY WHITTAKER and MIMI LAW
DON LANG
AND BIG SUPPORTING COMPANY

24th December

Pantomime 'Aladdin' starring comedians **Nat Jackley** and **Jimmy Clitheroe**.

1957

6th May

Comedian **Ken Dodd** appeared along with comedienne/singer **Joan Turner** (No further information).

5th August

The 'King of Skiffle' **Lonnie Donegan** starred along with up and coming comedian **Des O'Connor**.

12th August

Skiffle stars **Chas McDevitt & Nancy Whisky**, teenage rock'n'roll star **Terry Dene & The Dene Aces** plus singer **Edna Savage**.

23rd September

National Skiffle Contest

The Vipers on this tour included future Shadows Tony Meehan and Jet Harris.

Notes on programme made by Margaret Hobson of local skiffle bands in contest along with members names of The Chequers.

30th September

The American stars **Larry Parks** and **Betty Garrett**.

21st October

Sheffield Football Club's, Centenary Concert was held at the Empire on Sunday. For the concert they hired **Lonnie Donegan**, supported by **Colin Grainger**, singer and former Sheffield United player, plus local modern jazz ensemble **Savoy Quintet**.

28th October

Making a welcome return, the 'girl with a giggle in her voice', the sparkling singing star **Alma Cogan**.

11th November

Another appearance of comic **Jimmy James** and company. **Bretton Woods** and **Hutton Conyers**. Plus headliner **Dickie Valentine**.

25th November

2nd December

23rd December

Christmas Pantomime 'Little Miss Muffett' starring clowns **Charlie Cairoli & Paul**, **Henry Lyton**, **Sylvia Norman**, **Norman Caley**.

1958

31st March

Still maintaining a variety bill with dancers **Norman & Niki Grant**, ventriloquist more ariel thrills with the **Three Paulos**, comedian **Billy Stutt** and vocal and instrumental combo the **Hedley Ward Trio**. The second half featured **Norman & Niki Grant** again followed by comedy high wire act **Ron & Rita**, comic **Bill Waddington** and starring the glamorous **Alma Cogan**.

7th April

Saw hit parade star **Johnny Duncan** with his **Bluegrass Boys** headline a bill that also included the black British singing group **The Southlanders** and television comedian **Terry Scott**. Dance act **Gillian & June**, comedian **Freddie Earle**, 'feline capers' with the **Duo Russmar**, Continental jugglers **The Kordas**.

14th April

Another varied bill with **Rey & Ronjy**, crazy comedy duo **Nick & Charly Carta**, comedy acrobats **Manetti Twins**, singer **Jeff Lenner** and music and mirth makers **The Londonaires**, trick-cyclists **Vic Templar & Janette**, dynamic singing personality **Barbara Law** and the return of the golden trumpeter **Eddie Calvert**.

21st April

Starting with usual dance act with **Al Fuller & Janette** and followed by laughter makers **Vic Gordon & Peter Colville**, roller skating juggling act **Walthon & Dorraine**, new style comedian **Norman Vaughan** and television's exciting female singing personality **Yana**, portrait artist **Rhoda Diane**, romantic singing star of London's West End shows **Edmund Hockeridge**.

28th April

Moving with the times the Empire presented '**Stars Of 6.5 SPECIAL at the "2-I's"** featuring sensational new favourites from TV's Top Show including **Tony Crombie**, **Wee Willie Harris** and **Terry Dene**. Plus **Les Hobeaux Skiffle Group**.

16th June

'**Peaches Takes Off**' with, **Eno** and **Gray**, **Alan James**, **Joan Winters & Guy Fielding**, **Paul King**, **Glyn Thomas Trio**, **Duncan Sisters**.

23rd June

30th June

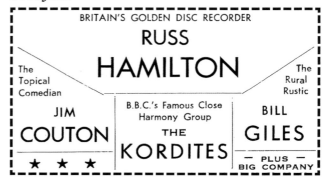

28th July

4th August

60

25th August

'A Girl Called Sadie' a kitchen-sink styled stage-play.

1st September

Latin-American show **'Tropicana Cuba'** with Cuban entertainers **Johnny Cha-Cha** and **Mercedes Hermanez** plus comedian **Hal Monty** and the **Alexis Troupe**.

15th September

The stage production of the musical **"Lilac Time"** starring **Walter Midgely** (No further information).

30th September

FOR ONE WEEK ONLY
THE DYNAMIC STAR PERSONALITY
of "THE JOLSON STORY" and
"JOLSON SINGS AGAIN"
LARRY PARKS
with
THE HAYWIRE FILM COMEDIENNE
BETTY GARRETT
and
FULL SUPPORTING COMPANY

13th October

Starring singing star **Shirley Bassey** (No further information).

29th October

Featured a return of the popular singing star **Dickie Valentine**.

2nd March

A comedy show starring three popular acts from stage and television **Jimmy Wheeler**, **Chic Murray** and **Joe Church** (No further information).

9th March

The Croft House Amateur Operatic Society staged their final show at the Empire with their version of **"King & I"**. (No further information).

16th March

PH!!!P HINDIN & CHARLES MUNYARD
present
CECIL SHERIDAN
"The Rogue with the Brogue"
and an All Star Irish Company
"IRISH & PROUD OF IT"
with
THE KILMURRY IRISH PIPERS & DANCERS

23rd March

Starring singer **Mr. John Hanson** in a production of the popular romantic musical **"The Student Prince"** (No further information).

30th March

Carroll Levis brought another of his talent shows "TV Star Search" also on the bill was actress and future successful authoress **Jackie Collins** (No further information).

6th April

A return for comedian **Frankie Howerd** who had first played the Empire in 1948 and was now starting to make a name for himself. Plus **Billy Tasker** in a production of the **Lilac Domino**.

13th April

PROGRAMME

Week commencing MONDAY, APRIL 13th, 1959

GEORGE and ALFRED BLACK
present
A New Spectacular Revue
"TOP OF THE TOWN"

1 OVERTURE ... ... *The Empire Orchestra*
under the direction of OWEN WALTERS

2 "CLOWNS IN CLOVER"
The Clowns ... The John Tiller Girls
and Terry Fearis
The Jesters .. JIMMY JEWEL & BEN WARRISS

3 "DIAMOND BRACELET"
THE JOHN TILLER GIRLS
Dance arranged by Barbara Aitken

4 HOLLANDER & HART ... *A Boy, a Girl, a Guitar*

5 "LINE ENGAGED" ... ... By Hills and Green
The Husbands ... ... JEWEL & WARRISS
The Wives ... Terry Fearis and Kay Woodman

6 CHARLY WOOD and partner *Comedy Juggler on the Unicycle*

7 THE IRIS ROY TRIO ... *Elegance in Dance*

8 "ROMANCE IN DANCE TIME"
The John Tiller Girls
Terry Fearis
introducing
JIMMY JEWEL and BEN WARRISS

INTERMISSION
Selection—"Night and Day"—*Cole Porter*
THE EMPIRE ORCHESTRA
Under the direction of MAURICE NEWTON

PROGRAMME CONTINUED OVERLEAF

FULLY LICENSED BARS IN ALL PARTS OF THE THEATRE

PROGRAMME
Continued

9 "STEPPING HIGH" ... ... The John Tiller Girls
Terry Fearis

10 "THE LONG BAR" ... ... By Hills and Green
with JIMMY JEWEL and BEN WARRISS

11 JOHNNY LAYCOCK and BEE *Crazy Music With a Sting*

12 TV's GLAMOROUS SINGING STAR
JILL DAY

13 "KEEP 'EM LAUGHING"
JIMMY JEWEL & BEN WARRISS

14 "TOP OF THE TOWN" ... ... The Company

Manager and Stage Manager		... ... ALEC MYLES
Carpenter	For	... WALTER WOLSTENHOLME
Electrician	"TOP OF THE	... ... KEN MILLAR
Property Master ...	TOWN"	... ... CYRIL ROLLS
Wardrobe Mistress ...	Company	... ... PEGGY BARRY-JAMES

PLEASE NOTE—PHOTOGRAPHING IN THIS THEATRE IS FORBIDDEN

The Management reserve the right to refuse admission to this theatre, and to change, vary or omit, without previous notice, any item of the programme

20th April

Singing star **Lupino Lane** and daughter **Lauri Lupino Lane** in a show titled **'Me & My Girl'**.

27th April

Singer and funny man **Max Bygraves** appeared along with singer/comedienne **Joan Turner**.

2nd May

The very last show at the Empire and starring again the popular comedian **Albert Modley**. Prior to the show Albert had his photo took showing him gazing thoughtfully round the theatre himself. Along with **Albert** the final bill included compere **Reggie Dennis**, musical clowns **Earl & Elgar**, spectacular knife-throwing act **Big Chief Eagle Eye** and the young ladies of the **J W Jackson Dancers**.

MORE AUTOGRAPHS FROM THE EMPIRE

(Top Row) Joseph Locke, Eddie Calvert, The Five Smith Brothers (2nd. Row) Rose Murphy, Morecambe & Wise, David Whitfield (3rd. Row) Alfred Marks, Ann Shelton, Vic Oliver (4th. Row) Norman Evans, Frankie Vaughan, Dave Morris (Bottom Row) Cardew Robinson, Beverley Sisters, The Radio Revellers With Grateful Thanks to Charles Johnson and Ann Chesney

Famous comedy duo's who appeared at the Empire in the 1950s

above: Ernie Wise and Eric Morecambe
below: Oliver Hardy and Stan Laurel

Empire
THEATRE SHEFFIELD

chapter five

The Performers

Chapter Five

The Artists

Comics & Comediennes

With their own and often unique style of comedy, the names would include both established performers and up and coming talent, many of which had enjoyed further popularity on television.

Extremely popular with radio listeners through his weekly radio show **Al Read** (1909-1987) would take a varied 'look at life' through the different characters he'd portray from the cocky and loud-mouthed to the meek and timid. He would also read snippets from the local papers and comment on them as part of his act. Unfortunately, what had been successful on radio, his style of comedy failed to have much effect on a live audiences. **Fred Emney** (1900-1980) was a big rotund performer who frequently appeared on TV and briefly in films in the 50's. With his trademark monocle and cigar he came across as the retired colonel type and would usually make some hilariously dry quips and asides in response to the actions or words of one of his assistants. He also played the piano and a speciality was a torrid version of The Flight Of The Bumble Bee.

1 Al Read
2 Fred Emney
3 Jimmy Clitheroe
4 Max Wall
5 Max Miller

In contrast to Emney, the pint-sized **Jimmy Clitheroe** (1921-1973) became a popular radio and television star playing the part of a boy due to his small stature and undeveloped voice. It was probably because of this that **Judd Newton** recalls being took by surprise when he saw Jimmy in a near-by Sheffield pub. "I was in the Adelphi, it was dinner-time and I saw this little bloke sat on a bar-stool. I said 'How do pal' and he said 'how do father or summat like that'. I said 'tha'at Jimmy Clitheroe aren't tha?' and he said 'Aye, I am'. He looked like a little kid sat there." Born James Robinson Clitheroe near Nelson, Lancs, Jimmy became highly popular on radio through his weekly shows 'Call Boy' and 'Clitheroe Kid', which he also enjoyed a series on television with. It is probably from this show that he's also remembered for, for his catch-phrase 'Eee, don't some Mother's 'Ave Em' ", which was later transformed into the title of the popular TV sitcom. 'Some Mother's Do Ave Em' starring Michael Crawford.

With his colourful stage-suits **Max Miller** (1894-1963) was usually billed as The Cheeky Chappy, due to much of his comedy being quite near the knuckle for its time. However, he would usually start his act by asking the audience what kind of jokes they wanted, "from the red book, or the blue book", it was more often than not from the latter.

Another Max was manic funny man **Max Wall** (real name Maxwell George Lorimer, 1908-1990) who along with singing and dancing would also feature his musical comedy alter-ego 'Professor Walloffski'. As this character he was somewhat mad looking, sporting shoulder-length hair, black tights and large leather boots in which he would cavort around the stage. Sat at the piano he would make it look as if one arm was shorter that the other and pull it out until they looked the same along with other silly antics. At the sound of drumming, he would then do a silly walk around the stage, although it was possibly an indication of how agile he was.

Another exponent of the 'funny walk' was the wonderful, **Nat Jackley** (real name Nathaniel Tristram Jackley Hirsch, 1908-1988) and he was also known as 'Nat the Rubber Man' as he would run round the stage and stretch his neck out as though it was made of rubber and with his little moustache he would look quite gormless.

Freddie Frinton (real name Fred Hargate 1908-1968) usually appeared dressed in top-hat and tails whilst his starched collar was generally scew-wiff, as he played the part of a drunken husband coming home late and looking rather dishevelled in his evening dress and crooked top hat and a broken cigarette dangling from his lips and uttering his catch-phrases of "good evening occifer" to the local Bobby or "'ave you seen my wife?" However, despite his convincing portrayal, in real-life Freddie was tee-total. In the early 60's he enjoyed success as a plumber character in the television sitcom *Meet the Wife*, which ran for 40 episodes with his wife played by **Thora Hird**. The series is mentioned in the Beatles song *"Good Morning, Good Morning"* with the line *"It's time for tea and* Meet the Wife*"*. In 1963 Frinton appeared in the TV sketch *Dinner for One* as the butler who stands in for three make-believe dinner guests and had to drink whatever the guests should have drunk and as a result gets hilariously sozzled. Surprisingly this has since become a cult TV show on German television and bizarrely, watching the non-subtitled English language sketch on television subsequently has become a German New Year's Eve tradition, with the short seeing multiple repeats every year from 1972 onwards. Another performer whose act was playing the part of a drunk was one-time Scottish music-hall comedian **Archie Glen** (1929-1998) and was billed simply as 'Blotto'.

Charlie Chester (real name Cecil Victor Manser, 1914-1997) had become a popular radio personality with shows included *A Proper Charlie* and *That Man Chester*. Another series - which started out as a section of *The Charlie Chester Show* in 1950 - was the quiz *Pot Luck*, which was a bit like the 'Generation Game' in part with members of the audience participating in the various fun and games amongst other comedy sketches. In the 1960s he began presenting a record show on the BBC Light Programme, later BBC Radio 2. 1969 saw the start of his long-running radio show *Sunday Soapbox* which came from the BBC's Manchester studios. He opened the programme each week with the introduction "With a box full of records and a bag full of post, it's radio Soapbox and Charlie's your host!".

Another familiar face on TV in the fifties was **Tommy Trinder** (1909-1989) who was the original compere of the popular Sunday Night At The London Palladium shows. **Charles Johnson** recalls Tommy at the Empire,

"Tommy Trinder brought his own company up. This was just as television was taking off. One night he played to a small audience and when they started to applaud him, he said, 'Stop, turn the lights on' and turned to the audience and said, 'there are more people up on stage than in the audience, so we will applaud you!'" Unfortunately, after cracking some tasteless jokes about illnesses on air, Tommy was replaced as Palladium compere by actor Robert Morley..

Terry Scott (1927-1994) was one of the young up and coming comedians in the 50's who was also a fairly frequently seen face on television. During this part of his career he also made his popular children novelty record of "My Brother". He would go onto enjoy regular major television exposure firstly with the comedy series 'Hugh and I' with fellow comedy actor Hugh Lloyd and later the extremely popular 'Terry & June' with comedy actress June Whitfield.

Another name who later enjoyed great popularity on television was **Benny Hill** (real name Alfred Hawthorne Hill, 1924-1992). His stage appearances usually featured him in sketches with members of his company. His subsequent TV success also spilled over onto records with novelty songs like "Gather In The Mushrooms", "Transistor Radio", "Harvest Of Love" which gave him chart status in

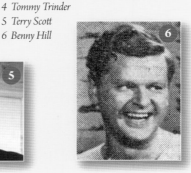

1 Nat Jackley 4 Tommy Trinder
2 Freddie Frinton 5 Terry Scott
3 Charlie Chester 6 Benny Hill

the early 60's all of which were written by Benny himself and not forgetting "Ernie (The Fast Milkman In The West)" which gave him another hit in 1971.

Comedian/actor **Jack Douglas** (1931-2008) was one of the Empire's supporting acts in March 1956 prior to forming a brief comedy partnership with Joe Baker. Jack then went onto create the character with the funny nervous affliction, Alf Ippititimus, and a regular face in many of the 'Carry On' films.

Another star of the Carry On films was lanky **Bernard Bresslaw**. (1934-1993) He first came to prominence as Private 'Popeye' Poplewell in the popular TV comedy series 'The Army Game' and even enjoyed a modest chart hit with his novel recording of "Mad Passionate Love".

Usually wearing his customary Tam O'Shanter, Scottish comedian **Chic Murray**, (real name Charles Thomas McKinnon Murray, 1919-1985) would be very droll as he quietly poked fun at his diminutive female co-star Madie as she sang at the top of her voice, seemingly oblivious to Chic's comical asides.

1 Bernard Bresslaw   *5 Hylda Baker*
2 Chic Murray   *6 Norman Evans*
3 Jimmy Wheeler   *7 Old Mother Riley-Kitty Mcshane*
4 George Formby   *8 Arthur Lucan*

With his catch-phrase of "Ay-Ay That's Yer Lot!" and customary trilby hat, cockney comedian **Jimmy Wheeler** (real name Ernest Remnant, 1910-1973) would also feature some melancholy violin playing in between his wise-cracks. In fact, Jimmy sometimes found it hard to either play the violin or deliver the punch-line as he was laughing too much.

Without doubt one of the most famous comedians to appear at The Empire was **George Formby**, (1904-1961) the dopey looking ukulele playing lad from Lancashire. He had in fact followed in the footsteps of his father George Sr. who had also appeared at the Empire back in the 1920s. With a number of films to his credit George had certainly become a superstar of stage and screen and was obviously a massive draw at whenever he played in Sheffield, although it's a safe bet that he always had his wife Beryl keeping a watchful eye on him.

Hylda Baker (1905-1986) was of course the demure little lady who usually wore a two-piece suit topped of with a fox-fur and usually accompanied by a six-foot tall man in drag. The stooge named 'Cynthia' remained silent throughout the act and only usually answered anything that Hylda said by an exaggerated nod. This would prompt Hylda to acknowledge her with her famous catch-phrase of "she knows y'know". Also in Hylda's act she would often get words and phrases that sounded like each other mixed up with great hilarity.

Someone else who would usually appear in drag was **Norman Evans**, (1901-1962) another wonderful Lancastrian comedy character. Well known for three sketches, with his most famous one being in drag as gossip 'Fanny Fairbottom' in 'Over The Garden Wall'. His others were 'At The Dentist' and an amusing routine with a little glove puppet panda called Teddy, which was something very similar to that of Harry Corbet's popular glove puppet Sooty. Interestingly, Norman Evans still holds the record for the longest-running pantomime ever, 'Humpty Dumpty' which ran at the Leeds Theatre Royal for 22 weeks in 1944-45.

Another truly wonderful comedy character drag-act was **Old Mother Riley**, played of course by **Arthur Lucan** (real name Arthur Towle, 1885-1954). Arthur's partner in the act was his wife **Kitty McShane**, (real name Kathleen McShane, 1897-1964) although their marriage and professional life together was a very stormy affair. This was mainly due to, whoever played the young man in their sketches would often become Kitty's current boy fiend and would flaunt him in front of everybody, including Arthur. Sadly, in view of this, Arthur turned to drink for solace which at times got the better of him. After Arthur died in May

1954, Kitty reclaimed the act and used Arthur's stand-in **Roy Rolland** (1921-1997) to play the part of Old Mother Riley and in fact did it as good as Arthur. **Charles Johnson** recalls their relationship. "Kitty McShane, she had a foul temper." The last time Arthur Lucan appeared at the Empire he was working on his own without Kitty. **Charles Johnson**; "He (Arthur) was at the Empire one week and she was at Doncaster. The word came from backstage that if she turned up at the Empire, she was to be chucked out by the scruff of her neck if necessary! Arthur was frightened to death that she would come causing trouble."

Nicknamed "the women's answer to Harry Secombe', powerful singer and comedienne **Joan Turner** (1922-2009) would mix operatic singing with her four-and-a-half-octave soprano voice with comedy and would easily turn a serious operatic piece into a funny one-liner accompanied by a very devilish look. Often ad-libbing with her audiences, it was not unusual for her to start singing *This is My Beloved* (from *Kismet*) only to break off with remarks like "Eee — look at the dust in here!". She became one of the highest paid entertainers in the 60's & 70's.

Another comedy character was **Arthur English** (1919-1995) who would usually make his stage entrance pushing a wheel-barrow on which would be an assortment of items he's supposed to be selling. Billed as 'King of The Wide Boys' he would usually be decked out in a long drape jacket with wide shoulders, trilby and a large, flashy tie complete with a pencil-thin moustache and sideburns, emphasising his 'wide-boy' spiv look. In his act Arthur would also appear with his son Anthony who would usually dress up similar to his Dad.

Considered something of a 'new wave' comedian in the 1950's **Frankie Howerd** (1917-1992) (real name Francis Alick Howard**)** went onto to be become another major star of stage and television. In the late 40's he had been a regular on the BBC radio show Variety Bandbox. In 1954, he made his screen début opposite Petula Clark in the low budget mystery comedy film The Runaway Bus, which had been written for his specific comic talents and was an immediate hit, although he never became a major film star. With his sarcastic wit and his double-entendres Frankie would often use his audience as part of his act. Someone else he would make fun of was his accompanying lady pianist as he would shout across to her the song he was going to sing as if she was deaf, and, turning towards the audience, he'd offer up a sympathetic "poor soul"!

Fred Karno's Army went back to the early musical hall days and was a total comedy experience and featured **Fred Karno** (real name Frederick John Westcott, 1886-1941) a one time theatre impresario of the British music hall. He was a pioneer in slapstick comedy and is credited with inventing the custard-pie-in-the-face gag. Among the young comedians who worked for him were Charlie Chaplin and Arthur Jefferson, who later adopted the name of Stan Laurel. In 1913, Karno had the Astoria houseboat built for him on the River Thames at Brentford, Middlesex, at a cost of £20,000. It was sold after he was made bankrupt in the late 1920's. It is now used as a recording studio by Dave Gilmour of Pink Floyd. In the 50's a latter day touring version of Fred Karno's Army appeared at the Empire and featured comedy act **The Four Graham Brothers**. To those of a certain age "Fred Karno's Army" is an almost forgotten term used in the UK to that occasionally refers to a chaotic group or organisation.

Another of the newer comedy acts of the 50's were brothers **Mike & Bernie Winters** (real names Michael,1929 and Bernie Weinstein 1932-1991). Changing their stage name to The Winters Brothers, they were not successful at first, and went their separate ways for a time. After reuniting, in 1955 Mike and Bernie as appeared for the first time on television, on the BBC show called Variety Parade.

1 Joan Turner
2 Arthur English
3 Frankie Howerd
4 Mike and Bernie Winters

The show was an undoubted hit for both the BBC and the act. The brothers remained with the show until 1958. Being a young act they toured with Tommy Steele and were also seen on shows like 6-5 Special and also in the film of the same name.

Character actor **Bernard Miles** (1907-1991) would come onstage pushing an old cartwheel, dressed in an old Farmer's smock and with a piece of straw in his mouth.

1 Harry Secombe   3 Stan Stennett   5 Jimmy James
2 Vic Oliver   4 Norman Wisdom

With a deep west-country accent his act was made up of humorous tales and observations of the people who made up the rural countryside where he was supposedly from. **Stuart Turton** remembers some of Bernard's countryside humour ; "he used to be telling someone 'have you 'eard that old Ben Turby had died?' Asked when did he die, his reply was, 'Well, come next Tuesday, he'll have been dead two weeks'!"

Both singer and funny man in the 50's **Harry Secombe** (1921-2001) was probably known in the latter role with his participation in the offbeat comedy series The Goon Show. Although it was often hard to take him seriously, the small Welshman certainly had a powerful singing voice and would include opera and popular ballads in his act made which made him another popular variety star of both stage, radio and television.

Another Welshman and musical comedy performer **Stan Stennett** (1925) was also an actor and jazz musician playing guitar and trumpet. As a comedian he would play whilst singing funny songs, emphasised with humorous vocal effects and comical facial expressions. He became a regular face on television when he was chosen as one of the regular comedy guests on The Black and White Minstrel Show. He also played straight acting roles in television programmes such as Coronation Street and Casualty. He was perhaps best known to armchair viewers for his long run as Sid Hooper in the top rating ITV soap opera, Crossroads, before taking a lease on the Roses Theatre in Tewkesbury, Gloucestershire, England, in 1980. Now in his eighties, Stan is still performing on stage.

Norman Wisdom (1915) became a huge favourite of both children and adults through his stage and especially film appearances. Originally a straight-man for magician David Nixon, he adopted the character 'the Gump' with his ill-fitting suit and flat tweed cap. In this role, he went on to develop his own highly physical knockabout act. Also a singer and songwriter, Norman's signature song was of course "Don't Laugh At Me Because I'm A Fool".

Vienna-born **Vic Oliver** (real name Victor Oliver von Samek, 1898-1964) was both a superb comedian and superb classical violinist.. With his dry sense of humour Vic would pretend to play the violin badly (similar to Les Dawson's piano playing) whilst breaking off to make wisecracks. He married Winston Churchill's daughter, Sarah, in 1936, but was divorced in 1945. He was also the first castaway subject on the Radio series, Desert Island Discs.

Another popular northern comic was **Jimmy James** (real name James Casey, 1892-1965) who was usually seen onstage puffing away on a cigarette whilst trying to cope with his two half-wit stooges and doing so had developed one of the funniest stage routines in variety history. Unfortunately Jimmy was a chronic gambler and could easily gamble his week's wages shortly after receiving them. This was probably a contributory factor towards Jimmy constantly suffering from ulcers. One of his stooges was the tall, lanky **Eli Woods** (real name Jack Casey & was James' nephew,) known as 'Our Eli' he had a permanently dopey look and would ask "Is it you that's putting it about that I'm barmy?" The other stooge was **Hutton Conyers**, played by members of the Casey family and more notably from 1956 to 1959 by a young **Roy Castle** (1932-1994) who would act equally as dopey. Offstage, Roy's initial job at any theatre was to usually find a nearby shop that provided chicken sandwiches for Jimmy. Jimmy James named the character of Hutton Conyers after seeing a signpost on the Great North Road to the small village of Hutton Conyers, north-east of Ripon in Yorkshire.

British born **Dickie Dawson** (real name Colin Lionel Emm, 1932) was one time the envy of many a British male when he was the husband of film actress Diana Dors. Dickie appeared at the Empire as a comedian. **Eric Kalman**; "He was a stand-up comedian, like Bob Hope that sort of thing and immaculate in his dress, always a silk suit and he was a really nice person. He was Jewish and when he came here my late mother used to make him Salami sandwiches."

Special mention should be made of comedy duo **Jimmy Jewell** (real name James Arthur Thomas Marsh, 1909-1995) and **Ben Warris. (1903-1993)** They were cousins, (their mothers were sisters) and both born in Andover Street, Pitsmoor, Sheffield and in fact they were born in the same bed —Ben in May 1909, Jimmy on Dec 4th., 1912. In the late 40's and early 50's their daft comedy routines were extremely popular as was their radio programme 'Up The Pole'. They became national stars on the variety theatre circuit and television too and were both very proud of their Sheffield links.

1 Roy Castle
2 Ben Warris and Jimmy Jewel
3 Eli Woods

Songbirds & Crooners

Singing songs of love and romance with the occasional novelty item, all the top female singers of the day were popular with audiences young and old at the Empire.

Sultry-eyed Liverpool-born songstress **Lita Rosa** (real name Lillian Patricia Roza, 1925-2008) had previously been the girl singer with The Ted Heath Band along with Dickie Valentine. Remembered for her novel hit "How Much Is That Doggie In The Window" which in fact she recorded with great reluctance and refused to sing ever again. Her other recordings included "Allentown Jail", "Idle Gossip", "Hernando's Hideaway" and "Volare". By 1955 Lita was a star in her own right and appeared at The Empire in June of that year.

Unfortunately, Lita was most annoyed one night when the show had to be stopped as recalled by **Charles Johnson**, "because somebody had died in the audience!".

1 Lita Rosa
2 Lita Rosa Review
3 Alma Cogan arriving in Chesterfield meeting the crowd
4 Alma Cogan and Jeff Blackburn cutting the ribbon at Jeff's new electrical shop in Chesterfield.

LITA ROZA
" Joey "
" Idle Gossip "
(Decca F.10335)

I'VE heard Lita sing a lot better than she does on " Idle Gossip," and somehow she just misses on this very lovely song. At times she sounds rather tired and a little out of tune—which is something really staggering for this on-the-note singer.

This is not a bad record, but it is not up to the usual Roza standard. Roland Shaw and his Orchestra give excellent support with a most tasteful backing and this record could have been a great one.

" Joey " is better, and a slight touch of echo has brightened Lita's voice. Like "Idle Gossip" this is a lovely song and rarely will a singer find two better pieces of material.

Both are possibly a little uncommercial, although in the case of "Idle Gossip" the public have already indicated their approval by putting it well up the Top Twenty list.

Tagged *'the girl with a laugh in her voice'* was **Alma Cogan** (1932-1966) the happy-go-lucky songstress was also known for her vivacious stage dresses. In the mid 50's Alma was also a regular member of the popular radio series 'Take It From Here' and as well as providing some musical entertainment she would also provide the occasionally heard voice of the 'Mrs. Glum' character. She became a popular live performer through her recordings like "Bell Bottom Blues", "I Can't Tell A Waltz From A Tango", "Twenty Tiny Fingers", "Never Do A Tango With An Eskimo", "Whatever Lola Wants", "You Me & Us", "Willie Can" and "Last Night On The Back Porch". Her success would also lead her to enjoy her own weekly television show. **Jeff Blackburn** has a special memory of when Alma came to the Empire. "It was March 1959 and Alma was appearing there for the week. I had already opened my own electrical shops in Sheffield and Rotherham, (Modern Electrics) and was about to open one in Chesterfield. So I went to the Empire to ask if Alma could come and open my new shop as showbiz stars did in those days and she was a number one star then. I walked into her dressing room and said 'hello' and then told her what I'd gone there for. She sat and thought about it and after we'd negotiated a fee (£50) she agreed to come and open the shop. On the following Saturday I went and picked her up at the Grand Hotel where she was staying as guest of Empire Manager Johnnie Spitzer.

On the way into Chesterfield all the roads were blocked with people and traffic trying to get into town. I went and asked a policeman what all the fuss was about and he said it's because some idiot has got Alma Cogan to come and open a shop'!!! I said 'you better come and look who's in my car' and when he saw who it was the police gave us an escort into town to the shop. After Alma had cut the ribbon for the shop there was so many people there the police said 'you've got to get her out as it causing too much chaos.' So I drove Alma back to Sheffield where I took her and Johnnie Spitzer out for lunch to the Grand Hotel. She was great".

Another popular vivacious female singer who appeared at The Empire in the mid 50's was **Eve Boswell** (real name Eva Keleti, 1922-1998). Born in Budapest, Hungary, the bubbly songstress enjoyed nationwide success in the UK between 1955 and 1956 with infectiously happy sounding hits like "Sugar Bush" and "Pickin' A Chicken".

Blackpool born **Joan Savage** (1930) may be vaguely remembered as one of the regular faces on the 50's pop show 'The Jack Jackson Show', usually appearing alongside her musical/comedy partner and husband Ken Morris. Joan recorded in her own right too having a version of "Love Letters In The Sand" released.

Blonde-haired beauty **Joan Regan** (1928) was another hugely popular female recording and television star of the 50's. On record her output included versions of "If I Give My Heart To You", "This Ole House", "Love & Marriage" and "May You Always". Today Joan Regan lives in Kent and continues to make stage appearances, many for charitable causes

Hailed as a possible British rival to Marilyn Monroe, **Yana** (real name Pamela Guard, 1932) and originally known as Yana Castle, traded a potential career as a 50's fashion model for a career in showbiz. Although she never achieved any big success on disc the sultry looking blonde was a regular face on numerous stage and TV shows. Her most famous hit was "Climb Up The Garden Wall" which made her a popular attraction at The Empire.

Anne Shelton (1923-1994) was another 'forces' favourite' and very popular singer of the 50's, remembered for her recordings of "Arrivederci Darling", "Lay Down Your Arms" and "Village Of St. Bernadette".

Remembered as one of the co-presenters of the 50's TV musical quiz 'Spot The Tune', **Marion Ryan's** (1933-1999) early career saw her as the petite vocalist with **The Ray Ellington Quartet**. She later progressed to becoming a recording star in her own right and had cover versions of US hits "Hot Diggity", "Why Do Fools Fall In Love" and "Stairway Of Love" and enjoyed a chart hit with "Love Me Forever" in 1958. **Stuart Turton** remembers seeing her outside the Empire stage-door. "I got her

autograph and then I asked her 'can I give you a kiss?' to which she replied, 'Oh no, I don't kiss anybody'!" Marion is also the mother of 60's pop twins Paul and Barry Ryan.

ANNE SHELTON
"If I Give My Heart To You"
"Goodnight. Well, It's Time To Go"
(HMV B.10745)
THESE two sides featuring Anne Shelton are a little below her usual high standard. She has the help of the Ken Mackintosh Orchestra, but for once the recording engineers have given us a rather poor balance, and the result is that the brass lacks the normal bite. Anne sings "Goodnight" a little slower than most singers, but the song lacks the type of melody that allows a singer to use any degree of feeling. In fact, it is a rather cold effort.
The reverse is also below standard and Miss Shelton sounds just a little tired. Also why on earth Ken's alto was kept so much in the background. I don't know. Here was a chance to make a great side, but it has not worked out very well.

1 Eve Boswell
2 Joan Savage
3 Joan Reagan
4 Yana
5 Marion Ryan
6 Anne Shelton
7 Anne Shelton Review

By the end of the 50's **Shirley Bassey** (1937) had become one of Britain's most promising female performers. The dusky eyed Welsh songstress had enjoyed some hit parade success in the 50's with "Banana Boat Song", "Fire Down Below", "Kiss, Me Honey, Honey, Kiss Me" and "As I Love You". Onstage she looked very evocative dressed in tight slinky, often quite revealing, stage costumes that certainly caught the eye of many of the males in the audience. Indeed, John Firminger recalls going to see Shirley at the Empire in '59 with my pal Richard when we both found her anatomy just as appealing as her voice.

Although she was born in England, film actress, singer and dancer **Julie Andrews** (real name Julia Elizabeth Wells, 1935) is more commonly known for her role in American film successes "Mary Poppins" and "Sound Of Music". It was while she was still an up and coming child radio star that she appeared at the Empire in 1953, billed as 'Britain's youngest Prima Donna'. The possessor of an extraordinarily high soprano voice, Julie had apparently been discovered singing for wartime crowds sheltering in London's underground stations.

1 Shirley Bassey
2 The Beverley Sisters, Babs, Joy and Teddy
3 Ruby Murray
4 Julie Andrews

The Beverley Sisters consisted of eldest sister Joy, (real name Joycelyn, 1929) and twins Teddy (real name Hazel, 1932) and Babs (real name Babette, 1932) and were daughters of George Arthur Chinery and Victoria Alice Miles who were known as Music Hall act 'Coram & Miles'. With their bubbly personality, the three sisters were equally popular with theatre and television audiences as well as on record with titles like "Sisters", "I Saw Mommy Kissing Santa Claus", "Green Fields", "Nylon Stockings" and "Little Donkey". In July 1958, in a well publicised wedding, Joy married captain of England's football team Billy Wright.

Somewhat dramatic Welsh-born vocalist **Dorothy Squires** (real name Edna May Squires, 1915-1998) included "A Lovely Way To Spend An Evening" and "I'm In The Mood For Love" amongst her recordings and onstage she was accompanied by her partner, songwriter Billy Reid on piano. That is until of course she went on to marry a young actor and ex male model by the name of **Roger Moore**.

Irish songbird **Ruby Murray** (1935-1996) dominated the UK charts during 1955, having at least one single in the charts for 52 weeks without a break, and in March she had five songs in the Top Twenty during the same week with "Heartbeat", "Softly, Softly", "Happy Days And Lonely Nights", "Let Me Go Lover" and "If Anyone Finds This I Love You".

 Another singing sister act, **The Tanner Sisters** were vocalists Stella and Francis. With recordings like "Ricochet", "Make It Soon", "Jealous Heart" and their version of "Green Door". Whilst at the Empire **Charles Johnson** offered the duo a suggestion; "As a joke I told them, why don't you sell your autographs for a tanner! (6d, 2.5p)." The duo would go onto earn themselves a bit of pop history having toured with the great Buddy Holly on his one and only British tour in 1958.

Both new names and established ones, in view of their popularity both on records and television many of these male performers found favour with both female and male members of the audience whenever they appeared at The Empire.

Standing at over six feet tall, Irish tenor **Joseph Locke** (real name Joseph McLaughlin, 1917-1999) was a most commanding performer onstage and a very popular attraction having become famous for his version of "I'll Take You Home Again Kathleen". Often seen accompanied onstage by his Great Dane, his rendition of "Soldier's Dream" would be most compelling. **Charles Johnson**; "Joseph Locke loved to sing and you couldn't get him off stage. He had to be virtually dragged off at the finish," **Charles** explains why the Irishman's act had to be curtailed, "This was because most of the attendants and backstage lads were milkmen and had to be up at 5.00am, so they didn't want to miss the buses or trams home." Joseph Locke would later become infamous for his income tax problems. This would subsequently lead him to appear with the more discreet name of 'Mr. X'. However most people were well aware of his real identity and this subterfuge only seem to enhance his appeal.

One of Britain's most popular singers of the 40's and 50's was crooner **Donald Peers** (1908-1973) whose famous signature tune was "By A Babbling Brook". He appears to have been a regular attraction at the Empire and many people,(probably including Peers himself), were quite surprised when he enjoyed belated chart status in 1968 with his recording of "Please Don't Go" and then again in 1972 with Give Me One More Chance".

G.H. Elliot (1882-1962) was also known as the 'Chocolate Coloured Coon', a name that certainly wouldn't be acceptable in these times. However for G.H. it was seen as a compliment for his vibrant singing style, which would imitate some of the black singers from the American deep south, similar to Al Jolson. George Henry Elliott was born in Birmingham but after his family immigrated to America he became a child star. However, they returned to Britain in 1894 and he began his spectacular rise to the top of British variety. Having encompassed some of the music of the Deep South, he would also black-up onstage to as a further compliment to the black singers he'd heard growing up whilst his songs also reflected this with titles like "Moonshine Is Better Than Sunshine", "On The Mississippi", "Down Home In Tennessee" and "Knockin' On Dixie's Door" although his most famous song was of course "Lilly Of Laguna". Also a superb soft-shoe dancer who, at times, appeared to be dancing on air. In variety he enjoyed phenomenal success for many years and made one of his final appearances at the Empire.

Famous for his singing **Ronnie Ronalde,** (real name Ronald Charles Waldron, 1923), was equally known for his bird-like whistling. While singing he would incorporate this into his songs such as "If I Were A Blackbird", "I Leave My Heart In An English Garden" and "Happy Whistler". Upon his return to The Empire in August 1951 he also featured some yodelling along with his bird impressions in his act.

A big attraction of the 50's was Hull-born **David Whitfield** (1925-1980). He got his first big break through Hughie ('Opportunity Knocks') Green who helped to get David a spot at the Washington Hotel in London. It was here that Decca Records heard him and signed him to the label. With his wavy fair hair, good looks and striking, almost operatic, vocal style he will probably be best remembered for his recordings of "Bridge Of Sighs", "Rags To Riches", "I Believe", "The Book", "Answer Me" and of course "Cara Mia". At the height of his career his live

1 Josef Locke
2 Donald Peers
3 G H Elliott
4 Ronnie Ronalde
5 David Whitfield

appearances broke box-office records at theatres all over the country and naturally made him a big draw at The Empire. **Patricia Raffo** remembers meeting him; "I have memories of, going to see David Whitfield and Joan Reagan in 1956 or 1957. I was a fan of both these artists. However I managed to go to the stage door and hand David Whitfield a rather large box of chocolates. He was pleased so much that he told me he had to watch his weight and thanked me for the thought."

1 Ronnie Hilton
2 Colin Grainger
3 Jimmy Young
4 Pearl Carr and
  Teddy Johnson
5 Tony Brent

Hull born **Ronnie Hilton** (real name Adrian Hill, 1926-2001) was yet another one of Britain's popular male singers in the 50's. He enjoyed a string of successes on record which included "I Still Believe" "Yellow Rose Of Texas", "Young And Foolish", "A Blossom Fell", "Who Are We?", "Around The World", "The Wonder Of You" and "No Other Love". He also recorded the children's novelty song "A Windmill In Old Amsterdam" which also resulted in another place in the Hit Parade. **Colin Grainger** (1933) was another young singer who had the distinction of also being a professional footballer. Prior to singing he played football, beginning in 1950, for Wrexham, Sheffield United, Sunderland and Leeds amongst other teams. Grainger became a recording artist, signed to the HMV label with a couple of releases "Are You"/"This I Know", "Love Only Me"/"Plain And Simple Girl". He also performed onstage, including an appearance at the Empire. During his time as a footballer he was known as 'the singing winger' due to his vocal talent and also billed as 'the voice with a kick in it'!. He subsequently concentrated on football and went on to be capped by England.

As well as his singing career, **Teddy Johnson** (real name Edward Victor Johnson, 1920) also had the distinction of being one of radio's first so-called 'disc-jockeys' when he would host his own weekly record show on Radio Luxembourg. This was during the early 50's when he presented the first 'top twenty' programme, then based on sheet music sales. Dapper-looking singer **Teddy** would often appear alongside his wife and singing partner **Pearl Carr** (1923). **Charles Johnson** remembers the young couple prior to their marriage, "Their relationship was on and off. Teddy told me he didn't know what to do, so I told him to marry her!" As a duo they are perhaps best remembered for their 1959 Eurovision song hit "Sing Little Birdie". Another popular hit parade star of the 50's was **Jimmy Young** (real name Leslie Ronald Young, 1921) who enjoyed great successes with his recordings of "Eternally", "Too Young", "Unchained Melody" and "The Man From Laramie". Billed as 'King Of The Discs' he was naturally a big attraction at the Empire.

With his slight Mediterranean vocal style **Tony Brent** (real name Reginald Hogan Bretagne, 1927-1993) was another popular vocalist of the 50's to appear at The Empire. He too had a succession of hits in the British hit parade with his recordings of "Walking To Missouri, "Make It Soon". Got You On My Mind", "Cindy Oh Cindy", "Dark Moon" and "The Clouds Will Soon Roll By".

Known for his relaxed singing style **Michael Holiday** (real name Norman Alexander Milne, 1924-1963) was also often compared vocally to the great Bing Crosby. On record he had success with "Hot Diggity", "Gal With Yaller Shoes", "Ten Thousand Miles", "Stairway Of Love", "The Story Of My Life" and "Starry Eyed". His singing voice was also heard on the television puppet series 'Four Feather Falls'

The smooth Irish singer **Ronnie Carroll** (real name Ronald Cleghorn, 1934) first appeared at the Empire in a show called Hollywood Doubles in which he blacked-up and performed as Nat King Cole. He also became popular on TV and records in the 50's with his recordings of "Walk Hand In Hand" and "The Wisdom Of A Fool" and later in the 60's with "Ring-A-Ding Girl", "Roses Are Red" and "Say Wonderful Things". He also attracted further attention when he married well known female singer Millicent Martin.

Blackpool born **Gary Miller** (real name Neville Williams, 1924-1968) was another popular balladeer of the 50's with his slightly dramatic versions of "Garden Of Eden", "The Story Of My Life", "Yellow Rose Of Texas" and "Robin Hood" and later on he was the singer heard on the theme song "Aqua Marina" as featured in the Puppet animation series 'Stingray'.

Another handsome balladeer and regular face on television was **David Hughes** (real name Geoffrey Paddison, 1925) whose records included "By The Fountains Of Rome" and "Bridge Of Sighs".

Dynamic singing star **Lee Lawrence** (real name Leon Siroto, 1920-1961) was another of the popular British male singing stars with his vocal version of "The Blue Tango" whilst he also made the spoof recording 'Rock'n'roll Opera'.

Whilst the majority of the British crooners and balladeers were pretty tempered in their approach and presentation, one of the first British acts to arouse any kind of hysteria amongst the young fans was singer **Dickie Valentine** (real name was Richard Brice, 1929-1971). The son of comedian Dickie Maxwell, his live performances always drew massive crowds wherever he appeared. During the 50's and 60's he enjoyed great success with his recordings of "A Blossom Fell", "Christmas Alphabet", "All The Time And Everywhere", "In A Golden Coach", Finger Of Suspicion", "Mr. Sandman", "Old Piana Rag", "Christmas Island", "A Teenager In Love", "One More Sunrise" and "Venus".

Another performer who was pretty charismatic was **Frankie Vaughan** , (real name Frank Abelson, 1928-1999). Boasting a healthy looking physique and good looks he was naturally a hit with the women especially when wooing them with his signature song "Give Me The Moonlight (and leave the rest to me)". From up-beat novelty items like "Tweedle-Dee", "Seventeen" and "My Boy Flat-top" Frankie would go onto have hits with "Garden Of Eden", "Green Door", "Kisses Sweeter Than Wine", Wanderin' Eyes" and "Kewpie Doll" that appealed to both youngsters and their parents. Through the songs he chose to sing his career developed into him becoming a much loved all-round performer very much in the suave hat and cane variety.

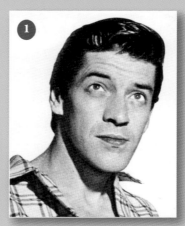

1 Michael Holiday
2 Ronnie Carroll
3 David Hughes
4 Dickie Valentine
5 Frankie Vaughan

Pop Back In The 1950's

David Whitfield and Joan Regan admire the gold record of " Cara Mia," presented to David to mark the million sales of the disc.

MY TOP TEN

By DAVID HUGHES

I ALWAYS thought that it would be easy for me to pick my ten favourite discs. Now I know better! For I think I must have a thousand and ten favourites instead of just ten. However, here they are:

YOU'RE RIGHT, I'M LEFT, SHE'S GONE, by Elvis Presley: I think that every Presley disc is the most but I single out this one because of its catchy title. What I like about Elvis is that he radiates masculinity.

SWINGIN' DOWN THE LANE, by Frank Sinatra: Just find a singer who doesn't think that Sinatra is the greatest! This track is from the wonderful "Songs for Swingin' Lovers" L.P. There's fine backing from the Nelson Riddle combo.

OUT OF AN ORANGE COLOURED SKY, by Nat "King" Cole: The velvet-voiced Nat is my wife's favourite vocalist so I just had to include him. I like his style, too, especially the way he sings this number.

THE GYPSY IN MY SOUL, by Eydie Gorme: Here's a young lady whose crystal clear voice must be a gift to the hi-fi engineers. I have always liked this song and Eydie's version is about the best I have come across.

ALL THE TIME AND EVERYWHERE, by Dickie Valentine: Dickie has a made-to-measure approach for ballads and this one is sung beautifully. It gets far more spins on my turntable than some of the current releases.

ANNA, by Anna Magnani: This record always reminds me of the first time my wife and I went to Spain. It was a big hit at the time.

SEPTEMBER SONG, by Sammy Davis Jnr: What a wonderful entertainer is Sammy. Any song sounds superb the way he sings but hearing his disc of "September Song" gives me particular pleasure.

BATTLE OF NEW ORLEANS, by Lonnie Donegan: I think this is the best record Lonnie has ever made. He sings it with a great sense of fun and soon sets the feet tapping. A value-for-money platter, this.

GIDGET, by James Darren: This title song from the new film is particularly welcome because it's such a change to hear a new record that hasn't got triplets in it. The lyrics are original too.

SUMMERTIME IN VENICE, by Mantovani: I am just one of the millions to fall under the spell of the Mantovani strings. His gentle treatment of this lilting composition sets me thinking of my holidays.

Ventriloquists

A look at the performers who were usually accompanied by some well known little friends including some very popular entertainers along with some lesser known practitioners of the art of ventriloquism.

An act that unfortunately seems to have seen a decline in numbers is that of the ventriloquist. Usually a man who would master the art of speaking without moving his lips whilst throwing his voice so it would appear that his dummy would be the one speaking. This act was a most popular one during in the 50's, 60's and into the 70's. One of the popular names of the early 50's was **Canfield Smith** (1926-1990) whose dummy **'Snodgras'** was billed as 'almost human'

Albert Saveen (1915-1994) was also billed under just his surname and would be dressed impeccably in full evening dress. He had an assortment of dummies but his most famous one was of course the tiny little doll-like figure **'Daisy May'** who would speak with a soft high voice using a lot of "ooh's" and "aahs". Another doll in **Saveen's** act would be a dog that would continuously yap whilst another, this time, a *real* dog would just look on until it had had enough of the yapping and say in a low human voice "sha-dap!". This was done by the use of a false jaw on the dog connected to Saveen's hand and had a most surprising effect.

Peter Brough (1916-1999) became a house-hold name through his popular radio series 'Educating Archie' along with his famous dummy, supposedly a mischievous schoolboy **Archie Andrews**. However in hindsight, it's quite ludicrous to imagine a ventriloquist on the radio as he wouldn't have to hide his mouth from moving! In view of this Peter Brough wasn't that good and in fact audiences at the Empire complained about this.

'It's In The Bag' would announce **Arthur Worsley** (1920-2001) who had the distinction of remaining totally silent throughout his act whilst his somewhat over-bearing dummy **Charlie Brown** would do all the talking.

On the other hand, the ever-smiling **Terry Hall** (1926-2007) first appeared onstage as the 'Irish Ventriloquist' with a doll in the shape of Irish character **Mickey Flynn**. However in the 60's Hall became a house-hold name with his other creation **Lenny The Lion,** enjoying a weekly TV show of their own. Despite being hailed as 'king of the jungle' his opening catch-phrase was "don't embarrass me" conveyed by his bashful smile.

The suave **John Bouchier** would feature a coquettish mermaid figure named **Miranda** as well as a cheeky boy figure. He maybe also remembered for not using a doll at all but with grease-paint, he cleverly made a little face on his fingers and thumb and used this as a little character.

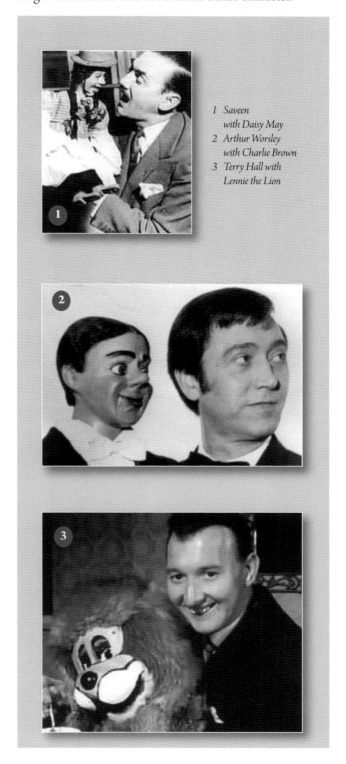

1 Saveen
   with Daisy May
2 Arthur Worsley
   with Charlie Brown
3 Terry Hall with
   Lennie the Lion

1 Bobbie Kimber
2 Dennis Spicer
3 Ray Alan

One ventriloquist who generated some controversy was **Bobbie Kimber** (1918-1993) aided and abetted by her little co-star **Augustus Peabody**. In her own speaking voice Bobbie would sound very genteel and lady-like but her cheeky companion's course, resonant male voice would be quite startling. However, all was revealed when one of the Daily papers exposed Bobbie as actually a man dressed up as a lady! Sadly this had an adverse act on Bobbie's career as it went into decline.

One of Britain's most underrated ventriloquists was **Dennis Spicer** (1936-1964) who came up with the very clever concept of throughout one of his TV shows would swap roles with his dummy. Doing this he became more wooden and animated whilst his doll, at the same time, became more and more human-like.

Johnson Clark (1886-1956) was one of the earlier vents with his little pal '**Hodge**' who came across as a country yokel.

Ray Alan (1930-2010) was one of the up and coming young 'vents' in the 50's and started out with a little character called '**Steve**'. Ray would of course go onto enjoy fame on stage and television in the 60's and 70's with his lovable characters '**Lord Charles**' and '**Tich & Quackers**'. Indeed, all these little characters earned a special place in our memories of seeing them both onstage and television. As well as being a 'vent' **Claude Chandler** would combine magic into his act. Billed as 'Your Family Ventriloquist'. Another forgotten name was **Archie Elray, Assisted by Dorothy**.

Instrumentalists

Popular and talented artists who specialised in various musical instruments who also appeared at the Empire

The number one pianist in the 1950's was probably Jamaican-born **Winifred Atwell** (1914-1983) who became hugely popular with her honky-tonk and boogie-woogie piano style. On record she had numerous successes with discs like "Coronation Rag" , "Black & White Rag", "Poor People Of Paris" and a series of "Let's Have A Party" recordings which featured medley's of current hit parade favourites. As well as her exuberant piano style Winnie's broad smile would always convey her friendly personality.

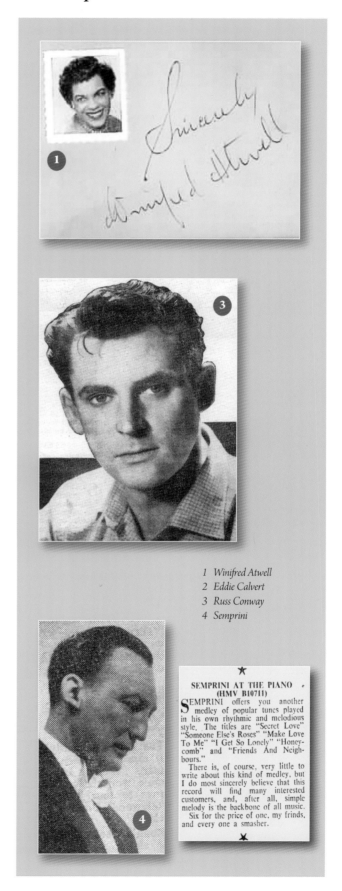

Hailed as 'The Man With The Golden Trumpet' Preston-born **Eddie Calvert** (1922-1978) became very popular through his recordings of "Oh Mein Papa", "Cherry Pink", "John And Julie" and "Zambesi". Pre-empting the craze for the guitars, Eddie certainly made the trumpet a popular instrument amongst the young. John Firminger states: "Before my teens, I used to have trumpet lessons given by one of the musicians actually from the Sheffield Empire orchestra"..

With his flashing smile another popular pianist was **Russ Conway** (real name Trevor Stanford, 1925-2000). Also employing a honky-tonk piano sound Russ enjoyed a succession of hit records with "Side Saddle" "Roulette" and "China Tea".

One pianist who had a great deal of class was **Semprini** (real name Albert Semprini, 1908-1990). A musician with great polish and would appear onstage in full evening dress. He was a very popular radio performer and would delight audiences with his superb playing on a variety of material that he would recall as "old ones, new ones, loved ones, neglected ones". Playing a variety of popular songs in a very sophisticated and most pleasing way.

The unassuming jazz pianist and acclaimed arranger **Bill McGuffie** (1927-1987) was another superb pianist and arranger who also made live stage appearances at the Empire.

1 *Winifred Atwell*
2 *Eddie Calvert*
3 *Russ Conway*
4 *Semprini*

★

SEMPRINI AT THE PIANO
(HMV B10711)

SEMPRINI offers you another medley of popular tunes played in his own rhythmic and melodious style. The titles are "Secret Love" "Someone Else's Roses" "Make Love To Me" "I Get So Lonely" "Honeycomb" and "Friends And Neighbours."

There is, of course, very little to write about this kind of medley, but I do most sincerely believe that this record will find many interested customers, and, after all, simple melody is the backbone of all music.

Six for the price of one, my frinds, and every one a smasher.

✖

1 Cherry Wainer
2 Tom Jacobson
3 Hedley Ward Trio
4 Harmonica Gang

Bubbly organist and singer **Cherry Wainer** became a familiar face on TV in the late 50's with her regular appearances on Jack Good's weekly television rock spectacular 'Oh Boy!'

A keyboardist of a somewhat futuristic kind was **Pierre Zampa** who back in the mind 50's played an Ondioline. This was a vacuum tube-powered keyboard instrument, invented in 1941 by the Frenchman Georges Jenny, and a forerunner of today's synthesizers.

Also frequently seen in variety shows on TV were popular musical act **The Hedley Ward Trio**, they featured pianist singer **Hedley Ward**, guitarist **Jack Mckechnie** and bass-player **Derek Franklin**. Bridging the gap between pop and swing they were and were featured on disc. Quite a slick act who performed with an ample amount of verve and enthusiasm as is evident on their a jazzy/swing cover of Rock Around The Clock and featuring a nifty solo from Jack Mckechnie.

On the humorous side of music one of the funniest acts was **Sid Millward & His Nitwits**. Similar to American band leader Spike Jones & His City Slickers, Sid's troupe of musicians also featured comedy routines performed by the various members of his crazy ensemble. Looking like a bunch of miss-fits dressed in an assortment of outfits from kilts, spats, evening dress and whilst they all acted like they didn't know what they were doing , their routines hid their true musical ability. One standout member of the band was their black drummer with a high-pitched voice **Cyril Kwango** and brother of famous wrestler Johnny 'Black' Kwango. Another black member of the Nitwits was **Dudley Heslop** who went onto become known as 'Cuddly' Dudley Heslop and was seen on Jack Good's 'Oh Boy!' TV show. A very popular act who were quite a spectacle, whether seen on television or on stage.

Sid Millward died in 1972.

Also mixing music and comedy were the **Morton Fraser's Harmonica Gang** and another act that was seen frequently on TV. The eight-piece group consisted of seven harmonica players, an accordionist and comedian. Members of the group at various times included **Dave King**,(1929-2002) the singer/comedian who acted as washboard player and stooge, **Don Paul, Gordon Mills**, **Ronnie Wells** and dwarf performer **Walter 'Tiny' Ross** who was generally the butt of some physical humour. As the group played a piece, he would keep trying to join in but get knocked out of the way by the backside of one of the group. Retaliating, Tiny would get a hat-pin and stick it in the guy's backside and then join in with the band!

Another popular harmonica act of stage and screen were **The Three Monarchs** who consisted of **Jimmy Prestcott** – Solo, **Eric York** – Chords and **Les 'Cedric' Henry** – Bass (1920-1986) who was the rather dopey member, although he was as much of a talented musician as his two compadres.

A most unusual musical act was that of pianist **Tom Jacobson** who had no arms, but instead played the piano with his feet. He would also sign autographs in this way too and was billed as 'The Armless Wonder'.

Possibly seen back in the early 50's as something of a musical novelty was **Mickey Ressel** billed as 'Electric Guitarist'. Indeed, whilst his act was perhaps ahead of its time and his name is long forgotten, his chosen instrument would certainly have a profound effect on popular music just a few years away.

American Legends

As well as all the top British artistes, Sheffielders were given the opportunity to see a number of touring American stars also came over to appear on the Moss Empire circuit and included visits to Sheffield.

1950 saw an appearance by the popular film and singing star **Allan Jones** (1907-1992) who had enjoyed great success with his recordings of "Donkey Serenade" and "Make Believe". He had also appeared alongside the Marx Brothers as straight man in their first two films "A Night At The Opera" and "A Day At The Races". He was also the father of singer Jack Jones. Another star of those films who appeared at the Empire was Marx Brother, **Chico Marx** (real name Leonard Marx, 1887-1961). **Eric Kalman**, "Chico Marx was just a superb person and he said to me, in his Italian accent, 'I teach you how to play the piano'. So he goes up right to the top octave and when he got to the top octave he'd play like that (holding his forefinger out like the barrel of a gun) and he'd say, 'see, you shoot the last key!'" Despite Chico's unorthodox style of playing, he was of course a world-class musician.

In June, 1952 the Empire saw a momentous appearance by the American film comedy double-act of **Laurel & Hardy** (real name Arthur Stanley Jefferson, 1890-1965 and Oliver Norville Hardy, 1892-1957) for the week from Monday 30th. June. In comparison their visit was likened to a visit by Elvis Presley, such was the world-status of **Stan** and **Olly.** Arriving at Midland Railway Station the duo were met by hundreds of people. Naturally their week's engagement at the Empire would be a sell-out as Sheffielders clamoured to see the legendary duo in the flesh. However **Eric Kalman** saw a side of Stan and Olly that he didn't like. "I met them with Johnny in the car park and they kept spitting everywhere. I couldn't stand that but in their culture they didn't realise it wasn't the thing to do." However despite this **Eric** found the two legends to be very nice indeed. "Oh superb. They each had their own limousine as they had brought their wives with them." **Charles Johnson** "They were very nice people, with no egos. Oliver called me 'Chuck' and gave me a signed photo." Onstage Stan and Ollie appeared in **A Spot of Trouble**, a sketch that took place in a small, remote, American town. The sketch was acted out in two separate scenes with the first on a railway station as **Carl Lodge** recalls. "I went to see Laurel and Hardy as a young lad with my mother. The backdrop for their act was a railway station platform in which they were both sat on a form, arguing over the fact that they had missed the train." **Eric Kalman** also recalls part of their act; "When Olly wanted to light his cigar, Stan simply reached up and bent this light over and lit it."

Of course the audience didn't know it was made of rubber and it looked quite something. Their act was sublime although I think the Sheffield audiences didn't understand their nuances and what had made them so successful." The second sketch took place in the living room of the Local US Chief of Police with Ollie and Stan in the roles of two travellers with the result being **'another fine mess'** as taken from their very famous catch phrase.

Ventriloquist **Ray Alan** has one special memory of working with the duo the night he got a knock on the dressing room door and opened it to find to his surprise it

1 Allan Jones
2 Chico Marx
3 Laurel and Hardy

was Stan Laurel who had a very large autograph book under his arm. Apparently, he got the autograph of every performer who he had ever worked with." Ray was so humbled, especially as Stan, now an old man, had trailed up three flights of stairs to get the autograph of an eighteen year old newcomer. **Carl Lodge**; "Stan and Ollie were both old men at the time."

American/Italian balladeer **Al Martino** (real name Alfred Cini, 1927-2009,) was a big hit in view of him having the distinction of topping the very first British charts, or Hit Parade back 1952 with his song "Here In My Heart" along with his other successes,, "Rachel" and "Now".

Another visiting act from the American and British Hit Parade were **The Four Aces** the smooth close-harmony vocal group consisting of **Al Alberts, Dave Mahoney, Lou Silvestri, and Rosario "Sod" Vaccaro**. The foursome enjoyed success on record with "Love Is A Many Splendored Thing", "Three Coins In The Fountain" and "Stranger In Paradise"..

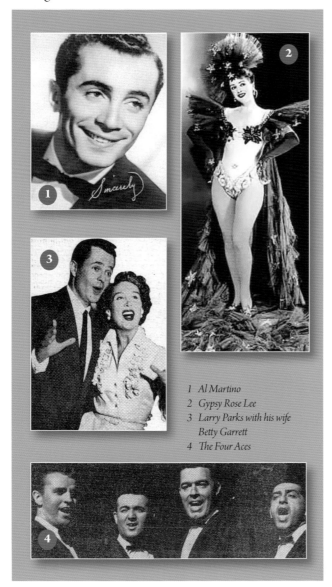

1 Al Martino
2 Gypsy Rose Lee
3 Larry Parks with his wife Betty Garrett
4 The Four Aces

Another smoothie was **Don Cornell**, (real name Luigi Francisco Varlaro, 1919-2004) billed as 'America's Great Singing Personality' he is possibly more remembered for his role as a slightly out-moded singing star in the rock'n'roll movie 'Don't Knock The Rock'..

FOR HIS FIRST VARIETY TOUR OF GREAT BRITAIN COMES
Tex Ritter
with another hit 'GREEN GROW THE LILACS' AND 'The Touch of the Master's Hand'
Capitol

Western hero at The Empire was singing cowboy **Tex Ritter** (real name Woodward Maurice Ritter, 1905-1974) With his days as a gun fighting hero of the silver screen now behind him Tex was treading the boards via the Empire Theatre circuit. As Tex was the star, the show had obviously been built round him as I (JF) remember the stage set resembled something like a western prairie. Also in keeping with the show's western theme the supporting cast included the male Canadian singing group **The Maple Leaf Four** and the **Morton Fraser Harmonica Gang**, both of whom I had seen on television. I recall Tex making a grand entrance on horse-back and spinning his lasso. Dismounting his act would consist of tales of the old west interspersed with some of his familiar cowboy songs like "I've Got Spurs That Jingle, Jangle" , "Green Grow The Lilacs" and of course "High Noon". Wondering how manager Johnny Spitzer coped with Tex's horse 'White Flash', **Eric Kalman** replied, "With a shovel!!!"

The famous 'Chee-Chee' girl **Rose Murphy** (1913-1989) appeared during her British tour in August 1953. Famous for her catchy recording "Busy Line" which she sang in an almost child-like voice. Unfortunately her unique style failed to make much of an impression on the Empire audience.

In contrast, the celebrated American striptease dancer **Gypsy Rose Lee** (real name Rose Louise Hovick, 1911-1970) was another notorious American who enthralled Sheffield audiences along with her **American Beauties**.

Another distant name from the film world is that of **Larry Parks** (real name Samuel Klausman Lawrence Parks, 1914-1975) who had enjoyed great success with his film portrayal of Al Jolson in 'The Jolson Story'. In September 1957 Larry performed an act of light comedy as well as a singing spot with his wife **Betty Garrett** (1919).

Speciality & Novelty Acts

Encompassing a wide variety of performers that would entertain by way of daring fetes of balance, strength, magic, trained animals or pure, unique talent

Raising a few eyebrows, the Empire would stage the occasional less family-oriented productions, consisting of nudity and glamour. Attendant **Charles Johnson** recalls these attractions with more directness , "Tits and bums took over from talent." These would include some of the French-style revue shows like **"La Revue Des Filles"** (*The Revue Of Girls)*, **"The French Peep Show"** (*A Real French Revue)* and the possibly less erotic **"Magicana"** (*featuring '25 breathtaking scenes' with 16 dazzling glamour girls)* **Une Nuit D'Amour** (Nudes De Desire). Generally featuring scantily-clad or nude young ladies these shows would often attract a mixture of young men and older ones from the '*dirty raincoat brigade'*. Another such production was 'Hello Burlesque' and featured nudity all the way, with **The New York Nudes**, **Broadway Lovelies** and **Burlesque Strippers,** interrupted only by comedian **Reg Varney** (1916-2008) who must have thought his birthdays had all come at once, working with such a show!

Back in those less promiscuous times these productions would often be looked down upon by the more '*respectable'* types. However, they were certainly an attraction to other less-inhibited people who would certainly relish what was on display and invariably get quite hot under the collar watching them, plus they usually gave people plenty to talk about at work the next day!

One young member of the audience was **Paul Walshaw**, "I had just started work in 1957 having left school in the summer. With a group of work colleagues I went to the Empire to see a strip show. Naturally as young teenage boys we were intrigued & fascinated at such a show never having seen one before. On the bill that night was British singer **Ronnie Harris** who had had a Top Twenty hit in 1954 with a cover version of Al Martino's U.S. hit "The Story of Tina". The show I seem to remember had lots of unclothed ladies doing what I suppose were burlesque acts tantalizingly covering themselves with very large feathers.

Another thing I remember was the sight of several statuesque smiling naked ladies posing in large metal cages suspended from the theatre ceiling. In those days the Lord Chamberlain decreed that the ladies could not move a muscle on stage'.

A Little less fortunate was **Terry Roe** from Darnall who would often go along full of hope of seeing plenty of young female flesh. Unfortunately for Terry he invariably found

himself sat behind one of the theatre's columns with a somewhat restricted view!

An act that possibly wouldn't be seen as politically correct today was **Burton Lester's Midget Show**, but a hark back to the days of Vaudeville and travelling freak-shows., Featuring ten 'Living Doll People' and also starring **Henry Behrens** the smallest man alive standing at just two and half feet tall who came onstage in a small coach pulled by a cat!

Colin Duffield recalls another Freak Show which featured the 9 ft tall Italian, **Sepatini** who included a boxing bout with a midget in his performance. "To publicise his appearance at the Empire his shirt and boots were on display in the window of Kings the dry-cleaners."

Equally freakish was another performer who had no arms but did things with his feet including firing a rifle. **Colin** "Another trick was dropping a box of matches and putting them all back in the box with his feet."

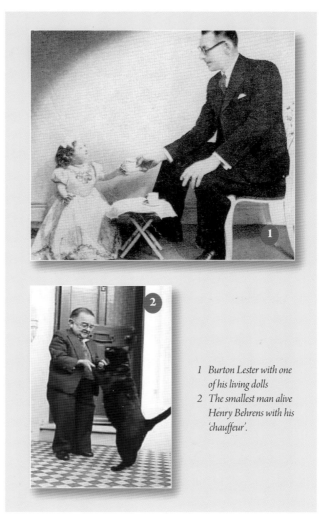

1 Burton Lester with one of his living dolls
2 The smallest man alive Henry Behrens with his 'chauffeur'.

A quite unique novelty act that most people of a certain age will fondly remember is **Wilson, Kepple & Betty**. Made up of Jack Wilson and Joe Kepple along with American Betty Knox who was later replaced by her daughter Patsy. However through the years there were a number of other 'Bettys'. Their eccentric dance routine would be billed as 'Cleopatra's Nightmare' with the two dog-faced male dances Wilson and Kepple doing a hilarious dead-pan Egyptian sand-dance whilst Betty looked on. The act retired in 1963.

A great comedy acrobatic act were **The Two Pirates** who were quite intriguing, firstly as they were outrageously dressed in small skirts with striped T-shirts and complete with Pirate Hats. Their act would see them perform a number of simple physical exercises as if they were nearly physically impossible. Then the highlight of the act was when the little one would run up the body of the bigger one and balance finger to finger. Jumping down to receive the applause of the audience he would stare quizzically out into the house, and say in a high pitched lilting voice, "Oh no there isn't..." as if he was reading the audience's thoughts. The audience knew what was expected and would shout back "Oh yes there is...". With a wistful simper, the little one curtailed the interchange.

"Its a *lie*..." with his voice going up at the end of the sentence. To emphasise the absurdity of the proposition. However, of course there was a wire- you could see it clearly in the lights and would be more obvious as the smaller Pirate hung in the air.

One novelty act who was always a big hit with children both on stage and television was **Windy Blow** (real name David Cecil). Dressed as a clown he would create various things out of balloons. Local musician **Bob Davis** recalls his

1 Wilson, Kepple and Betty

performance at the Empire; "I was one of the young kids who volunteered to help him onstage but every time it was my turn to receive one of his balloon animals, he'd send me to the back of the queue. After about the fourth time I was virtually in tears, unaware that he was actually using me in the act. Eventually there was only me left onstage and he gave me the most and the biggest balloons he could make. I felt really chuffed on the bus on the way home as I kept knocking people's hats off with all my balloons and look back on it as possibly my start in showbiz!"

Of course there were many acts that had audience participation with one being the Yorkshire Hypnotist, **Peter Casson**. Requiring a member of the audience to join him on stage. Attendant **Charles Johnson** recalls his own role in the act, "the attendant's job was to stand at the back of the hypnotised member of the audience. This was because, everytime the orchestra played "So Tired", the hypnotised person would fall asleep and the attendant had to make sure that if they were smoking, he took the cigarette out of their mouths!"

Magicians have continued to be popular to the present day and **Charles Johnson** remembers one particular magic act at the Empire; **The Great Lyle** (real name Cecil Lyle,) and his 'Cavalcade of Mystery'. "He was always sacking his staff, so if a member of his staff knew he was going to get the sack after the show, he would slow-time his tricks." **Charles** recalls one of the tricks, "He would put a man in a box and make him disappear and would then appear almost immediately up in the Gallery. He would do it by using identical twins." However, Charles recalls one occasion when, this trick was exposed, "This was given away by one twin having a pair of brown shoes on and the other had black shoes! This had been seen by a member of the audience who had brought a large pair of U-Boat binoculars." As well as being superstitious, Lyle was also a hypochondriac and if anyone sneezed near him he would immediately rush off to his dressing room.

Animal acts always seemed to be a popular inclusion on any variety bill although none of them ever rose to great heights. An assortment of four-legged friends would generally demonstrate, on command from their trainer, various levels of intelligence as they performed various tricks and routines. In these more politically correct times, acts such as these now seem almost unnecessary, however the animals themselves were usually well-looked after and generally displayed some pleasure in their performances as being part of showbiz.

Such acts included **Alexander's Dog Revue, Louise with her Dog & Pony. Darly's Dogs,** billed as 'The Canine Wonders' were featured in a sketch where the dogs stole some sausages from the village butcher. A little more dignified was **Duncan's Collies** who were billed as 'Canine Actors', ('Too bark or not to bark, that is the question'?) Moving up in size, **Derrick Rosaire** who presented his Wonder Horse **'Tony'**. Another equestrian act, billed as 'The Animal Act Supreme' was **Cook's Pony Revue.** An animal act of a different kind was **Bob Bemand & His Comedy Pigeons** and billed as 'Flying Funsters'.

Sounding like a couple of Hylda Baker's stooges were the balancing and juggling act **Cynthia & Gladys.** The final show at the Empire included some spectacular thrills with knife-throwing act **Big Chief Eagle Eye.** Also specialising in dangerous projectiles was **Rondart,** whose talent was displayed as the 'Champion Dart Blower'.

Someone else who was always a popular addition to a bill were the impressionists who would imitate well-known figures of the day. Two favourite impressionists who had been seen regularly on television were **Peter Cavanagh** and **Clifford Stanton.** Radio impersonator **Jackie Hunter** was billed as 'The One-Man BBC'. Similarly **Victor Seaforth** was billed as 'The Man With a Hundred Voices', whilst **Eddie Arnold** went one step further being billed as 'Mr. Everybody'.

One of the most unique acts was **Leslie Welch** (1907-1980) known as 'the Memory Man'. Possessing a real gift he could recall anything that members of the audience asked him for, whether it be sport, entertainment, war-time conflicts and news in general. In view of this he was an extremely popular attraction in variety shows.

Following in the footsteps of the great Houdini, and billed as 'the man they could not hang' **Alan Alan** (real name Alan Rabinowitz) invited members of the audience to come up onstage and try and stop him from escaping.

Trick cycling acts were also a popular addition to a variety bill with acts like **Annell & Brask** whilst **The Three Astons** went a step further with their act 'Football On Wheels' which combined football and cycling. Another cycling act with a touch of comedy were **The Wonder Wheelers,** billed as 'Laughter Peddlars'. 'Thrills on Wheels' were those of a different kind , announcing the **Skating Avalons** who would perform on a small round riser erected on the stage. Members of the audience were invited to participate, spinning round whilst strapped to a member of the act. Unfortunately those who did volunteer usually had to be attended to by the St. John's First Aid staff afterwards!

1 Leslie Welch
2 Joan Rhodes
3 The Mihailovits

A Strong Woman act which was billed as the **'The Mighty Mannequin'**, shapely blonde-haired strong woman **Joan Rhodes** had the 'body of a pin-up and the strength of a stevedore'. Her act included tearing up of telephone directories (with an estimated total of 20,000 during her career), bending iron bars in her teeth, round her neck and across her knee and throwing large men over her shoulder all of which made her a curious and popular attraction on stage and TV.

The **Mihailovits** were two Danish brothers who did a dynamic comedy/acrobatic balancing act, throwing each other around the stage.

The brothers always performed their act smartly dressed in bow ties and suits.

New Talent

As the Empire continued to book young talent, in doing so, it also reflected some of the changes evolving in the entertainment world

A popular attraction at the Empire was the frequent talent shows held which would feature up and coming local and national talent. Presenting the talent shows would be **Carroll Levis** (1910-1968) a Canadian who had become well-known in Britain for his television talent show '**Carroll Levis Discoveries**' on which a number of acts had achieved their first big break into show-business. In the hope of the same, his touring stage-show would attract various performers, young and old, to show what talent they had with The Empire providing the prestige. Auditions were held every Monday morning at 10 o'clock with adults and children queuing up for their chance of fame. Those who got through the auditions appeared onstage on one of the

1 *Marina & Elaine with Carroll Levis, at the Empire auditions 1951*
2 *On the bill at the Hackney Empire*

week's nightly shows which ran from Monday to Thursday with the final on Fridays. Saturday nights would feature a 'Saturday Night Pay-Off' with the winner being judged by audience.

One young performer who successfully auditioned for Levis back in February 1951 was **Elaine Marsh.** "My life long friend, Marina and I attended the Fayre Deviso School of dancing for 10 years, and were "discovered" by Carol Levis at the Sheffield Empire! We toured with him for 2 years (**'Elaine & Marina'**), I had to get permission from the education council to perform 'cos I was only 14yrs. at the time in my 4th year at High Storrs School. Marina is a year older and as soon as I was 15yrs we had to get in touch with Carroll, & our first date was at the Blackpool Palace.

Happy days!! We toured with Carroll Levis for a year playing all the Stoll & Moss Empire Theatres then he put a Teenage Show out playing all the second rate theatres, such as Attercliffe Palace. Violet Pretty compared the show and we all had a great time. Barry Took sometimes took over & Jim Smith was also with us, later known as Jim Dale! We then went on to join a Hungarian act called 'The Lacey Troupe, Acrobatic & walking on big Globes' for another 2 years. Pete Collins 'Would you Believe it Show' played at the Empire in 1954 I met my Husband touring with this show, he worked for "Vogelbein Bears". We've been married for 54 years in March!" Both Marina and Family and myself and Family are still living in Sheffield in Grenoside.

Another young local performer was singer **Mary Millar** who was born in Doncaster and educated at Shirecliffe in Sheffield. Her first professional engagement at the Empire, Aug 1950, singing operatic songs.

Also getting in on the discovery act was singer **Lee Lawrence** who, on one of his week's engagements at the Empire, organised a talent spot. Similarly organised with auditions throughout the week, two young performers would be selected top appear on each of the evening's shows and were given a chance to record for Decca Records.

Towards the end of the 50's, some of the acts featured in some of The Empire's shows would signal a new wave of entertainment and also the demise of the variety bill. Tastes were changing and teenagers had become a voice of their own through the clothes they wore, their attitude and most of all their music.

In order to keep up with the times The Empire would start featuring acts that would attract this new audience. The first signs of a youthful musical revolution was of course by way of skiffle music. Inspired by the 'king of skiffle' **Lonnie Donegan**, (real name Anthony Donegan, 1931-2002) it was basic form of acoustic music that many youngsters would find easy to get involved in with the requirements being a modicum of talent but plenty of enthusiasm. Centred around the guitar, or more than one if possible, other *instruments* would include washboards and tea-chest basses. In the wake of the craze, skiffle contests were being staged in various forms all around the UK. One of **Lonnie Donegan's** appearances at the Empire was also celebrating the centenary of the Sheffield FC.

Eric Kalman recalls Lonnie being quite upset one night when he came off stage. "I was in Johnnie's office and when it got to the interval, a very irate Lonnie Donegan came in. He said, 'John, somebody's hissing me'. Johnnie could hardly contain himself and I thought it was funny too. But being the manger, Johnny showed Lonnie some sympathy and calmed him down and said 'who's hissing you?'. Lonnie replied, 'I don't know but its somebody in the upstairs circle'! " **Eric** also recalls doing a 'favour' for Lonnie. "He was staying at the Grand Hotel, I remember the room as we were out in the car-park and I was chatting to John, saying 'cheerio'. Then this window opens and we heard 'Eric, Eric!' I'd arranged for him to have a girl, but he shouted 'don't bother about the girl, I've got one myself!'." Known as the 'king of skiffle', Lonnie is also remembered as quite a rude and insensitive person as **Pete Carson** recalled; "I met him after the show at a jazz club party somewhere up Howard Street and told him I had all his records to which he snapped back saying, 'what do you want, a medal?'."

A new talent mixing comedy and song was **Des O'Connor** (1932) who was regarded at the time as one of the brightest acts in variety. Mixing both novelty songs and ballads, Des obviously had a winning approach billed 'in the modern style'. In 1958 he became part of rock'n'roll history when he acted as singer/ compere on the one and only British tour of Buddy Holly.

Whilst 1957 was the year of the skiffle boom, it raged on nationally through 1958 and capitalising on it was London promoter **Stanley Dale** organising the Nation Skiffle Contest which would play theatres around the UK and in September 1958 it would take in the Sheffield Empire for the week. Acting as resident artists of the contest would be recording stars **Jim Dale** (real name Jim Smith, 1935) and **The Vipers**. Both acts had become famous via their television appearances on '6-5 Special' on which **Dale** had

become a teenage attraction with his records of "Be My Girl", "Piccadilly Line", "Just Born (To Be Your Baby)", "Crazy Dream" and "Sugartime".

The Vipers were one of the ensembles at the forefront of skiffle with their recordings "Don't You Rock Me Daddio", "Cumberland Gap" and "Streamline Train". They made an unsuccessful later attempt to switch to rock'n'roll with their half-baked cover of "Summertime Blues". Leader of The Vipers, **Wally Whyton** (1929-1997) recalls, "We were in the death of the Music Hall and we tended to do music hall most of the time with the sort of speciality act and the dancers. I must say it was a bit more interesting actually as we had chorus girls which was lovely!"

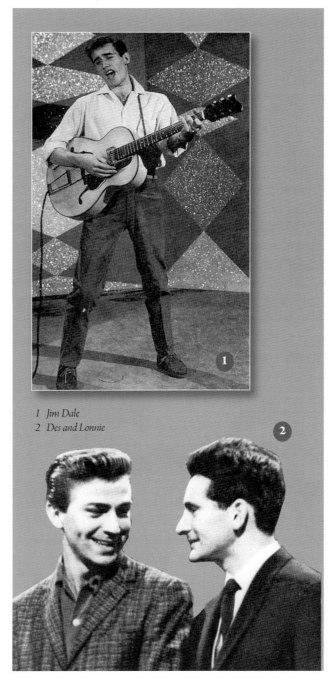

1 Jim Dale
2 Des and Lonnie

89

1 The Vipers
2 Lonnie Donegan advert
3 The Chequers
4 Advert for Johnny Duncan

Like it had done in other parts of the country, the 'National Skiffle Contest' would naturally attract young skifflers from all over the area with the event giving many a aspiring musician their first real public appearance. Amongst the many who participated were **Vic Cocker**, brother of Joe, and his band **The Headlanders**, **The Frantic Four**, **The Chequers** and **The Devil Chasers** (made up of three vicars!)

Jim Dale also acted as compere of the show and would also perform his own spot with **Wally Whyton** playing the guitar behind the curtain whilst Jim pretended to play his out front! Whilst Jim Dale was also a good organiser he was the first showbiz person **Jim Greaves** of The Chequers; had ever heard swear when he told the group if they didn't come onstage on time they'd get a 'bollocking'. "As 16 year-old lads it shocked us that these people used this sort of language."

Groups would take part every night with the finals talking place on Friday and Saturday nights. For both the promoter and the theatre this event turned out to be a great money spinner as it would bring in friends and relations of those taking part. Another participating skiffler was **Brian Fowler** of the Frantic Four; "We were obviously the best that night but there was this other group on with the tea-chest bass. This lad was skiffling away and he jumped on the tea-chest and it folded into a great big heap into the drum-kit and they won because of their exhibitionism". The finals saw the Barnsley quartet **The Moonshiners** become the contests' eventual winners, perhaps due to the fact that they'd brought several coach loads of supporters with them.. Whilst it was exciting for the entrants, the weekly contests became monotonous and depressing for **Wally Whyton** and The Vipers; "Practically every group would have a go at "Don't You Rock Me Daddy-O" and then at the end, we had to sing it too." **Hank Marvin** of **Shadows** fame played with the Vipers for a short while. The finals of the competition eventually took place in London at the Streatham Locarno.

Although he was associated with the skiffle craze, former Chris Barber band member and Tennessee-born ex-US service-man **Johnny Duncan** (1932-2007) was more closely connected to country music. After settling in the UK he became very popular through his recording of "Last Train To San Fernando", a fast train song that had been caught up in the skiffle movement. He formed his group **The Bluegrass Boys** who included dazzling guitarist **Denny Wright** and toured the theatres whilst following up with minor hits "Get Along Home Cindy" and "Footprints In The Snow"

Also getting in on the skiffle craze, **Carroll Levis'** discoveries show would also include a number of young Sheffield hopefuls with young groups such as The **Mainline Rhythm Group** and **The Rolling Stones** (nothing to do with the world famous band). However against some tough opposition from more experienced outfits, the group made it to the final of the Levis Show, despite guitarist Tony Lewis playing through their act with a dislocated arm. As a member of **The Black Cats Skiffle Group**, **Carl Lodge** was another entrant; "The first audition took place on a Sunday. We got to town on a bus with the tea-chest bass under the stairs. There must have been about 200 people there all trying to get through to the next stage of the talent contest. I received a letter a week or so later saying that we were through to the next round. This involved appearing on stage mid-week in front of an audience. The first three winners on each night went on to the Saturday night show and the winners on the Saturday night show went onto Caroll Levis's television show. We sang 'Rock Island Line' and came fourth on the night and thereby ended our show business career."

Other local outfits who took part on the **Carroll Levis** shows at the Empire included **The Twin Cities Rhythm Group**, **The Cross Rhythm Group** and **The Andy Capps** who had a picture of the cartoon character Andy Capp on their bass-drum! Member of the Andy Caps, **Pete Jackson** also has an 'outstanding' memory of the night, "a young Jackie Collins, and sister of Joan was there and showing quite a lot of cleavage. At first we went to the Empire as a country/skiffle band but after we saw her we became a jug-band!" The lady also made a big impression on **Carl Lodge**; "Before we went onstage a young woman in her early twenties asked us what we were going to sing as she was the compere. She was an absolute stunner and as lads of a young age, our chins were nearly touching the floor! The lady in question was Jackie Collins, her father, Joe Collins was an agent for Moss Empires."

Another teenage act that got it's big break on another TV talent show were **The King Brothers**. After being seen on 'All Your Own' the three brothers, **Mike** (guitar/vocals,1935), **Tony** (bass/vocals, 1937) and **Dennis** (piano/vocals, 1939) would appear on '6-5 Special' and began making records. Their recording career saw them achieve some success with their versions of US hits "A White Sports Coat (and a pink Carnation)", "Wake Up Little Susie" along with others like "In The Middle Of An Island", "Put A Light In The Window", "Standing On The Corner", "Mais Oui" and "76 Trombones". **Dennis King** recalls his days of touring the Empire circuit, "It was very much a situation that you did weekly Variety in each

town, you could do the same act. A lot of Variety acts went round touring the halls year in, year out just doing the same thing of course they were never exposed to TV. So they could kinda get away with doing whatever they'd done for years and there were enough theatres to play at. It was unlike the one-night stands and the subsequent rock'n'roll tours. There was much, I thought, sort of sense of camaraderie among the units that toured. 'Course you were usually in a show with half a dozen other acts who went from Sunderland to Newcastle or down to Hull or wherever. You would meet, I mean it was like a ritual, you'd meet Monday morning after band-call for a coffee at the local coffee shop and then decide your plans for the rest of the week, where you're stayin' in digs, who you're in digs with, what pictures are on, what you're gonna see, if you played golf, you'd go and arrange a game of golf or whatever. And there was much more a sense of unity about it. There fun of being in a theatre, particularly when we started and we were very young was this sort of excitement of feeling of being one of a group of touring players."

1 *The Mainline Rhythm Group*
2 *The King Brothers record*

Britain's first big rock'n'roll name in the 50's has to be **Tommy Steele**, (real name Tommy Hicks, 1936). His rise to fame was meteoric and became Britain's first answer to names like Bill Haley and Elvis Presley. Steele achieved his early success with hits like "Rock With The Caveman", "Elevator Rock", "Singing The Blues", "Butterfingers", "Cannibal Pot", "Water, Water" and "Handful Of Songs". **Maureen Burrows**; "I can remember Tommy Steele on stage in a yellow T-shirt and jeans singing 'Rock With The Caveman'. We were very impressed with his rock'n'roll.". As well as stage and television appearances he also starred in several films like the biographical 'Tommy Steele Story' followed by 'The Duke Wore Jeans' and 'Tommy The Toreador'. After the Cannibal pot went cold, Tommy's career developed further as he went onto become an all-round entertainer incorporating singing and dancing and moved on into stage and film musicals and a far cry from his rock'n'roll beginnings.

Also appearing at the Empire was Tommy's younger brother **Colin Hicks** (1940) who'd followed in Tommy's footsteps and also become one of Britain's young rock'n'roll stars. His band were called **The Cabin Boys** and included drummer **Jimmy Nichol** (1939) who later went onto stand in with The Beatles and Dave Clarke Five when their respective drummers were indisposed.

Marty Wilde (real name Reg Smith, 1939) was probably the next big name in those early rock'n'roll days. Along with his band The Wildcats who included future Shadows **Brian Bennett** (1940) and legendary guitarist **Big Jim Sullivan** (1941). With some early hits like "Honeycomb" and "Endless Sleep" he was another popular attraction at the Empire.

One of the first all-rock'n'roll packages to play The Empire was **'Stars Of 6.5 SPECIAL at the 2-I's'**. At that time the 6.5 Special, the BBC TV's first attempt at a Rock n Roll program. It was broadcast on Saturdays at five past six. .Featuring many famous artists of the time such as Lonnie Donegan, Tommy Steele and Petula Clark appeared on the show which was co-hosted by Pete Murray, a favourite DJ at the time and the show's co-producer Josephine Douglas..

One of the BBC's first live outside broadcasts to take place was on this show. It was from the 2-I's, coffee bar in London, the birth place of a number of young stars in the 50's.

One of the young stars of 6-5 Special was 15 year-old Scot **Jackie Dennis** (1943) With his covers of American hits of "La-De-Dah" and "Purple People Eater" he was billed at the Empire as 'the Lilt Of The Kilt' pertaining to the fact he always appeared in traditional Scottish dress.

On the same bill as Jackie at the Empire were another ensemble from the '6-5 special', **The John Barry Seven** led by York-born singer and trumpeter **John Barry** (real name John Barry Prendergast, 1933). The son of Cinema owner Barry's early composition "Hit & Miss" became the familiar signature for TV pop show 'Juke Box Jury'. The band had also made regular appearances on ITV's 'Oh Boy!' and the BBC's 'Drumbeat'. Other members of the band were singer **Keith Kelly** (1947), pianist **Les Reed** (1935) and guitarist **Vic Flick**.(1937)

Another regular from 6-5 Special who appeared onstage at the Empire was the Halifax born singing trombonist **Don Lang** (real name Gordon Langhorn, 1925-1992) who with his band, **The Frantic Five** recorded their own version of the TV show's theme song, with it's familiar opening; "Over the points, over the points".

Capitalising on both the popularity of 6-5 Special and The 2 I's, as well as signalling a new wave in entertainment, a stage show was devised and toured the provincial theatres of the time. The show would be obvious attraction for many local teenagers some of whom would heed the rock'n'roll call themselves becoming local heroes like **Dave Berry** (real name David Grundy) and **Frank White** who went to see the shows at the Empire and watched intently. **Stuart Turton** also watched the shows from up in the 'Gods'. "It was so steep though, if you rolled forward you could easily go over the top as the safety rail wasn't very high." **Stuart** also recalls some of the young couples on the front row and what could happen if the young girls didn't 'play ball' when the lights went down. "The blokes would take their ice creams off them and lob em' over the front and they'd land on somebody's head!"

Back up onstage, direct from London, the **2 I's-6-5 Special Show** featured **Tony Crombie & His Rockets**, **Wee Willie Harris**, **Jimmy Jackson**, **The Most Brothers** and **Terry Dene**. **Terry** recalls the shows; "Many of the Moss Empires which were showing the old Variety shows were beginning to have package-shows with just modern artists. It was all a new group of people, still a kind of variety of act but very much in the rock'n'roll bag." Prior to rock'n'roll, big bands had been highly popular it was from this area that some musicians were moving into the new musical trend.

One such musician was former jazz drummer **Tony Crombie** (1925-1999) whose ensemble had the distinction of being Britain's first rock'n'roll band. Taking a similar musical approach as Bill Haley & The Comets' sound, their repertoire included obvious contrivances of rock'n'roll like "Let's You & I Rock", "Rock'n'Roller Coaster" and "Shortnin' Bread Rock". In comparison to some of the big rock'n'roll package shows in America, this show could have been likened more to the Billy Cotton Band Show, but for the younger audience, it did provide something similar to their kind of music. One of the local performers who appeared that night was **John Driver**. "The time that I remember mostly is when I appeared on a show with Tony Combie, the pink haired Wee Willie Harris, Jet Harris (then a member of Tony Crombie's Rockets) and Jim Dale who compared the show. There was a feature for local talent to appear in the show and I was fortunate to be selected at the auditions to appear in the show. On the night Jim Dale introduced me and I walked on the stage with my guitar and amplifier and started Tommy Steel's "Handful of songs" that required the opening bars to be whistled - very difficult when you're scared stiff, but I managed to get through to the end of the song and got a good applause. Happy days for a young seventeen year though!!"

The two good looking **Most Brothers** were singers **Alex Murray** (real name Alex Wharton, 1939) and **Mickie Most** (real name Michael Hayes, 1938-2003) whose brief career on record together included covers of Marvin Rainwater's "Whole Lotta Woman" and "Whistle Bait" originally cut by US duo The Collin's Kids.

The pink-haired rockin' wild man **Wee Willie Harris** (real name Charles William Harris,1933) proceeded to run round the stage like the demented soul he purported to be and is vaguely remembered for his records of "Rockin' At The 2 I's", "Love Bug Crawl" and "Got A Match".

Terry Dene (real name Terry Williams, 1938) was one of Britain's brightest young talents following on in the wake of Tommy Steele. His records included "Stairway Of Love", "A White Sports Coat", "Start Movin'" and "C'Min & Be Loved" and starred in the British pop film 'The Golden Disc'. **Terry Dene** recalls working in Variety and it's transition to more youth-orientated shows . "When I started, I remember after doing the Moss Empires for a few months, I was working with people like Mikki & Griff, Larry Grayson and a number of sort of performers of that ilk. And to me Variety was really great fun working with these people at the time and you were actually pleased to be working with old-timers and they were usually a great bunch of people, we used to have great times in the theatres. But gradually these type of acts began to sort of, melt into the background as it were and the rock'n'roll thing came in full-steam, skiffle, rock'n'roll rhythm & blues and it began to flood the market so the other, old-time Variety just faded out."

Unfortunately Dene's career took a serious nose-dive when he was called-up for National Service and suffered a mental break-down. Dene was subsequently released from the Army on medical grounds but as a result suffered public humiliation and ridicule, leaving his once potential career in tatters. Thankfully Dene had the resolve, due to a new-found belief in Christianity, to overcome it all and today enjoys the status and respect of being one of the first great names of British rock'n'roll. Terry's appearance at the Empire was the second week of a big national tour. Bass-player with The Dene Aces was future member of The Shadows, **Brian 'Liquorice' Locking**, (1938) "That's where my career took off., it was the second week of a big tour, we'd just played Glasgow Empire before we went to Sheffield. We were on with a Canadian act, The Maple Leaf Four plus a comedian." Unfortunately, Terry's first appearance at the Sheffield Empire didn't go too well as **Brian** recalls; "He was upset about something on the first day at the Sheffield Empire and he walked off stage and left us standing there." It seemed like Terry had had some sort of anxiety attack and after a couple of numbers walked off **Brian**; "(Guitarist) Terry Kennedy had the wisdom to continue and carried on with the act and we did OK."

There were of course other names who cashed in on the rock'n'roll trend who appeared at the Empire. One performer who, although was never really associated with rock'n'roll, would perform in an exuberant style that would appeal to the younger generation was singer/ percussionist **Ray Ellington** (real name Harry Ray Pitts, 1916-1985). This would later lead him into make some rock'n'roll styled recordings like "Giddy Up A Ding Dong", "Green Door", "That Rockin' & Rollin' Man", "Left Hand Boogie", "Livin' Doll" (not the Cliff Richard song) and covers of US hits "Stranded In The Jungle" and "Charlie Brown". With his musical catch-phrase "That's Nice!", Ray was also heard regularly on the 50's cult radio programme 'The Goon

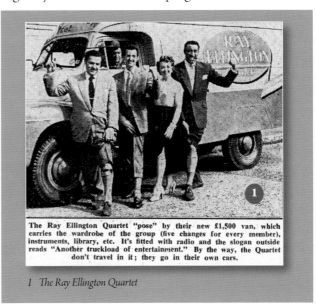

The Ray Ellington Quartet "pose" by their new £1,500 van, which carries the wardrobe of the group (five changes for every member), instruments, library, etc. It's fitted with radio and the slogan outside reads "Another truckload of entertainment." By the way, the Quartet don't travel in it; they go in their own cars.

1   The Ray Ellington Quartet

Show'. On it he would be featured both as a musician and as a comedy actor, taking part in many of the show's off-the-wall sketches.

Lead by lead vocalist Harry Douglas, black American vocal group **The Deep River Boys** always gave a lively performance of popular numbers. Based in the UK the group consisted of Harry Douglas (baritone), Vernon Gardner (first tenor), George Lawson (second tenor), Jimmy Lundy and Edward Ware (bass). They recorded cover versions of rock'n'roll hits "Shake Rattle & Roll" and "(We're Gonna) Rock Around The Clock" backed by Sid Phillips and his band.

Another similar act were **The Southlanders** who were a group of young Jamaican immigrants. Their line-up consisted of Vernon Nesbeth, Frank Mannah, Allan and Harry Wilmont who is entertainer **Gary Wilmot's** father. They too would capitalize on the sounds of their American counterparts with their recordings of US hits "Earth Angel", "Alone", "Torero" and not forgetting of course their novel hit and a favourite on BBC Radio's Light Programme 'Children's Favourites', "I Am A Mole (And I Live In A Hole)". Obviously a song of great social significance, they don't write em' like that anymore.

ROCKIN' AT THE EMPIRE

Tommy Steele

Tony Crombie & His Rockets

Wee Willie Harris and Johnny Duncan

Terry Dene

The Most Brothers

Pantomime & Musicals

A look at two of the Empire's most enduring types of shows

Always a popular feature of any theatre around the Christmas period time was the Christmas Panto. In fact, it's a good bet that it's the Pantos that many of you reading this book will remember above all. Usually staged around a well-known fairy story or nursery rhyme, the productions were written and staged by Emile Littler. Usually starring a well known personality of the day with an assorted cast of comedians, singers, dancers, etc.. In accordance with the story cast members dressed up in period costumes, with male members as dames and female stars often cast in the role of boys.

Traditionally, after rehearsals, Sheffield's, pantomimes first performances took place on Christmas Eve and despite the damage the Empire had suffered on December 12th. the theatre managed its first performance on the 26th December, 1944 after a mammoth effort of the staff.

Up-holding the tradition, The Empire had its share of some highly memorable pantos through the years with some lavish productions.

1952 saw comedian **Tommy Fields** star in **"Mother Goose"** along with **The Chevalier Brothers** and **Charles Warren & Jean** plus a *'big cast of pantomime stars'*.

The ever-popular **"Cinderella"** once again brought in the crowds, young and old for Christmas 1953 with it's star, the ever-popular northern comedian **Albert Modley** (1901-1979) and used real coach and horses.

The 1954 season had **"Goody Two Shoes"** headed up by **Sonny Jenks**, **Phil Strickland**, **Medlock & Marlowe** and **Beryl Stevens** all now sadly forgotten stars of yesteryear.

Christmas 1955 saw Emile Littler's production of **"Jack & Jill"** starring the popular radio and Television personality **Charlie Chester** ably supported by **Kathleen West**, **The Five Olanders**, **Sid Plummer** and **Lowe & Ladd**.

95

The Christmas 1956 Pantomime starred funny men **Nat Jackley** and **Jimmy Clitheroe** in the traditional tale of **"Aladdin"**. Nat played the traditional dame role of **Widow Twankie** and Jimmy was **Wishy Washy**. Another of the Christmas seasons **'Humpty Dumpty'** starred **Albert Modley** again as King Yoke of Eggvile (would his jokes be classed as 'wise-*cracks*'?) and featured **Pamela Grant** in the title role.

Babes in the Wood was The Empire's final panto and ran over the Christmas 1958 period. It was to feature newly weds **Edna Savage** and **Terry Dene**. However when Dene was called up for National Service, teenage singer Laurie London became the co-star.

Naturally these productions were mainly aimed at the children. Escorted by their parents making the event a family outing they would boo and cheer at the various

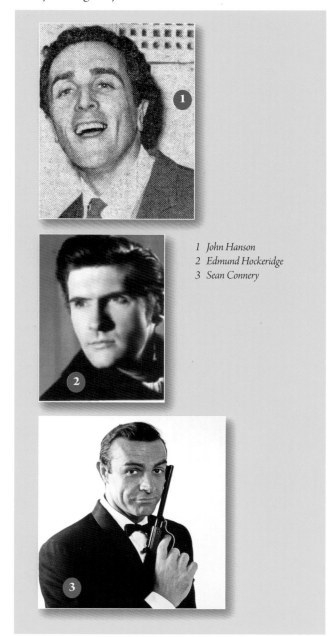

1 *John Hanson*
2 *Edmund Hockeridge*
3 *Sean Connery*

characters as they would play their respective parts, good and bad. Amongst all the drama and mayhem it would often be the parents who would end up enjoying the show often more than the kids – oh yes they would!

As the Pantos were usually aimed at younger audiences, they were usually presented twice daily with the first show at 2.30pm and one at 7.15pm.

Produced by Emile Littler, musicals would be another regular attraction with a variety of productions playing at the Empire for two or three weekly runs. **"Zip Goes A Million"**, billed as *'The Zippiest, Snappiest and Happiest Musical In* Town' was a show that had come from the Palace Theatre, London. Originally featuring **George Formby**, who eventually had to leave due to ill-health. His place was taken by **Reg Dixon** whose career then took off. **Arthur Askey**, the pint-sized star later took over but didn't want to go on tour with the show outside of London. Therefore the leading role for touring productions would be given to **Max Wall** and later northern comedian **Roy Barbour**.

When the ever popular Rodgers & Hammerstein musical **"South Pacific"** played Sheffield it included in the chorus line a young actor by the name of **Sean Connery** (1930). One afternoon it was arranged for the cast of the show to play a game of football with the team of milkmen who worked part-time as theatre attendants.

Another Rodgers & Hammerstein production was **'Carousel'** which ran for three weeks and starred suave Canadian singer **Edmund Hockeridge** (1919-2009). The spectacular musical **'The King & I'** was apparently made even more attractive when it played The Empire, being 'enhanced by the theatre's third dimension and living intimacy', wow!

With a run of three weeks, the oriental musical **"Chu Chin Chow"** was staged on ice with the Empire's stage covered with a special layer of ice. Wonder if the audience had to keep their overcoats on?, as there's no details of how cold the theatre had to be for this. Although some of the male dancers who took part in the shows may have looked quite soft and effeminate, **Charles Johnson** remembers some of them as otherwise, "The ballet dancers were very tough."

The Empire would also play host to some of the local productions. One of these was The Croft House Operatic Society. As **Charles Johnson** recalls, the company always showed the Empire staff how grateful they were, "They were lovely people and would give us 2/6 (12.5p) tip."

The Desert Song was a popular attraction with its star, the dashing male singer **John Hanson** (1922-1998). With his dramatic singing style he was known in particular for his role as the Red Shadow in the musical as remembered by **John Ward**. "All the ladies waived their handkerchiefs when he sang Good byeee."

Presented by London Striptease promoter Paul Raymond the show '**Las Vegas**' featured both live performers along with striptease girls and the voices of American stars via their records being played in stereo sound.

A musical production of a slightly different kind was '**Riders Of The Range**' which was based on the popular radio series of the early 50's. Written by **Charles Chilton** (1917) who also wrote the other popular radio series 'Journey Into Space'. Including some music the show was situated out in the west, the show featured acts in keeping with its theme and included knife-throwing act **Chief Eagle Eye** and also **Walter 'Tiny' Ross** the dwarf from **Morgan Fraser's Harmonica Gang** as Big Bill! plus **Don Cameron**. Yippee-Yi-Yay!

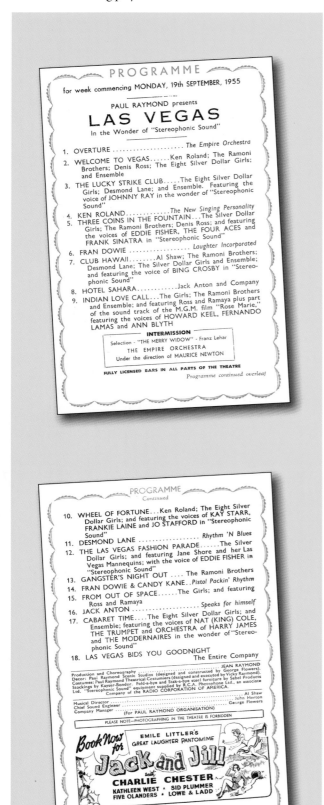

PROGRAMME
for week commencing MONDAY, 19th SEPTEMBER, 1955

PAUL RAYMOND presents

LAS VEGAS
In the Wonder of "Stereophonic Sound"

1. OVERTURE .... The Empire Orchestra
2. WELCOME TO VEGAS...... Ken Roland; The Ramoni Brothers; Denis Ross; The Eight Silver Dollar Girls; and Ensemble
3. THE LUCKY STRIKE CLUB..... The Eight Silver Dollar Girls; Desmond Lane; and Ensemble. Featuring the voice of JOHNNY RAY in the wonder of "Stereophonic Sound"
4. KEN ROLAND .... The New Singing Personality
5. THREE COINS IN THE FOUNTAIN... The Silver Dollar Girls; The Ramoni Brothers; Denis Ross; and featuring the voices of EDDIE FISHER, THE FOUR ACES and FRANK SINATRA in "Stereophonic Sound"
6. FRAN DOWIE .... Laughter Incorporated
7. CLUB HAWAII........ Al Shaw; The Ramoni Brothers; Desmond Lane; The Silver Dollar Girls and Ensemble; and featuring the voice of BING CROSBY in "Stereophonic Sound"
8. HOTEL SAHARA............ Jack Anton and Company
9. INDIAN LOVE CALL.... The Girls; The Ramoni Brothers and Ensemble; and featuring Ross and Ramaya plus part of the sound track of the M.G.M. film "Rose Marie," featuring the voices of HOWARD KEEL, FERNANDO LAMAS and ANN BLYTH

INTERMISSION
Selection - "THE MERRY WIDOW" - Franz Lehar
THE EMPIRE ORCHESTRA
Under the direction of MAURICE NEWTON

FULLY LICENSED BARS IN ALL PARTS OF THE THEATRE
Programme continued overleaf

PROGRAMME
Continued

10. WHEEL OF FORTUNE... Ken Roland; The Eight Silver Dollar Girls; and featuring the voices of KAY STARR, FRANKIE LAINE and JO STAFFORD in "Stereophonic Sound"
11. DESMOND LANE .... Rhythm 'N Blues
12. THE LAS VEGAS FASHION PARADE...... The Silver Dollar Girls; and featuring Jane Shore and her Las Vegas Mannequins; with the voice of EDDIE FISHER in "Stereophonic Sound"
13. GANGSTER'S NIGHT OUT ... The Ramoni Brothers
14. FRAN DOWIE & CANDY KANE .. Pistol Packin' Rhythm
15. FROM OUT OF SPACE...... The Girls; and featuring Ross and Ramaya
16. JACK ANTON .... Speaks for himself
17. CABARET TIME.... The Eight Silver Dollar Girls; and Ensemble; featuring the voices of NAT (KING) COLE, THE TRUMPET and ORCHESTRA of HARRY JAMES and THE MODERNAIRES in the wonder of "Stereophonic Sound"
18. LAS VEGAS BIDS YOU GOODNIGHT
The Entire Company

Production and Choreography .... JEAN RAYMOND
Decor: Paul Raymond Scenic Studios (designed and constructed by George Flowers).
Costumes: Paul Raymond Theatrical Costumiers (designed and executed by Vicky Raymond).
Stockings by Kayser-Bonder. Fold-a-bye and Stak-a-bye steel furniture by Sebel Products Ltd. "Stereophonic Sound" equipment supplied by R.C.A. Photophone Ltd., an associate Company of the RADIO CORPORATION OF AMERICA.

Musical Director .... Al Shaw
Chief Sound Engineer .... John Horton
Company Manager .... George Flowers
(For PAUL RAYMOND ORGANISATION)

PLEASE NOTE—PHOTOGRAPHING IN THE THEATRE IS FORBIDDEN

Book Now for EMILE LITTLER'S GREAT LAUGHTER PANTOMIME
Jack and Jill
with CHARLIE CHESTER
KATHLEEN WEST ★ SID PLUMMER
FIVE OLANDERS ★ LOWE & LADD

PROGRAMME
for week commencing MONDAY, MAY 18th, 1953

TEXAS PRODUCTIONS by arrangement with CHARLES CHILTON and by permission of the British Broadcasting Corporation present

RIDERS OF THE RANGE
(Based on the Famous Radio Series)

CHARACTERS IN ORDER OF APPEARANCE

MARY .... DOLORE WHITEMAN
HANK .... STAN KAYE
DON PEDRO .... DAVID KEAN
JEFF .... NORMAN HARPER
LUKE .... CHARLES IRWIN
RUSTLER (Himself) .... ROMULUS OF WELHAN
        P.D.(Ex) T.D.(Ex) U.D.(Ex) C.D. (Ex)
BIG BILL .... WALTER ROSS
DON .... DON CAMERON
CHIEF EAGLE EYE .... HIMSELF
COWBOYS, MEXICANS, INDIANS, etc.
SPECIALITIES by
MARIE DE VERE'S TEXAN BELLES
NORMAN HARPER and his HORSE "STARLIGHT"
THE FIVE MIGHTY MOHAWKS
MORTON FRASER'S HARMONICA GANG
Directed by JOHN WARRINGTON
SYNOPSIS OF SCENES
SCENE 1 .... JUANITA, A TEXAN BORDER TOWN
The Company
SCENE 2 .... HITTING THE TRAIL
SCENE 3 .... 6.T.6. RANCH
Luke, Big Bill and Rustler
SCENE 4 .... SOMEWHERE ON THE PRAIRIE
Mary and Jeff
SCENE 5 .... AN INDIAN VILLAGE
Chief Eagle Eye and Don Pedro THE MIGHTY MOHAWKS
SCENE 6 .... A CAVE IN THE ROCKS
Luke, Big Bill and Hank
SCENE 7 .... FORT DEFIANCE. RODEO
Jeff, "Starlight," Luke, Hank, Big Bill, The Texan Belles
MORTON FRASER'S HARMONICA GANG

INTERMISSION
THE EMPIRE ORCHESTRA
Under the direction of MAURICE NEWTON

FULLY LICENSED BARS IN ALL PARTS OF THE THEATRE
Favourite proprietary brands at Popular Prices
Whisky 2/-   Gin 1/9   Port and Sherry 2/-
Beers and Minerals at moderate prices
Programme continued overleaf

PROGRAMME
Continued

9. "RHYTHM ON THE RINK" .... No Rough Edges
The Ice Princesses
10. REG. MOORES .... Stunts on Stilts
11. MARY AND JIMMY SHERWOOD ...... Thrills and Spills for Laughs
12. LUBA NATOVA .... Skating for Your Delight
13. WONDROUS and MIMI .... Danse Apache
14. "THE BALLET OF THE ROSE" .... A Skating Dance Interpretation
Jean Colquhoun, Luba Natova, Pat Bowman, Martin Jakubait, Paul Stapleton, Bobby Brignell, Michael Arden, and The Ice Princesses
15. "THE TERRIBLE TWINS" .... Presented by JAN TORS
16. WILLIAMS and SHAND .... Up High from Down Under
17. "SLOW and SOPHISTICATED" .... In Modern Manner
Luba Natova, Pat Bowman, Michael Arden, and The Ice Princesses
18. "THE CHARLADIES" .... Speeding Up the Cleaning Up
Bobby Brignell, Paul Stapleton, Martin Jakubait, Jimmy Peacock
19. JEAN COLQUHOUN .... A Dance Medley of Scotland
20. "THAT'S ALL FOR NOW"......The Entire Company make their bows and hope you enjoyed the show
Goodnight, Good Luck, and Good Weather!

Music selected and arranged by Reginald Swinney.
Scenery designed and painted by Edward Delany and constructed by Show Properties Ltd. Costumes designed by Anthony Holland and executed by Dukes of Wardour Street and Theatrical Models.

Production Manager .... For .... LOUIS BARBER
Musical Adviser .... HOLIDAY ON ICE .... REGINALD SWINNEY
Press Representative .... (GREAT BRITAIN) .... FRED GRATTON
Chief Refrigerating Engineer .. LIMITED .... O. M. MATTHEWS

Manager .... For .... RON HACKNEY
Musical Director .... "CARNIVAL ON ICE" .. LESTER HOSKIN
Ballet Mistress .... COMPANY .... JOSIE CORDREY

PLEASE NOTE—PHOTOGRAPHING IN THE THEATRE IS FORBIDDEN

Bill Matter & Catch Phrases

Accompanying all the names on the various bills would be either a description of the act (sometimes quite lyrical) or sometimes a catch-phrase that a performer was either known for or had adopted for themselves and would compliment their names on posters and adverts, etc.. These few words would be known of course as 'bill matter' and looking back some of it appears both humorous and/or quite curious. The catch-phrase of the more well-known personalities would be more widely known but if some the lesser known performers would use some unusual catch-phrases.

1 Ann Shelton
2 Reg Dixon
3 Al Read

Bill matter for many performers tended to be a little predictable with 'Star of Stage and Screen' credited after their name. Female singers often had very similar billings with 'Girl and a Song' for **Jill Manners**, 'Golden Girl Of Song' for **Janie Marden**, **Joan Regan** was billed as 'The Queen Of Song', **Lynda Ross** was the 'Sweetheart Of Song' whilst **Ann Shelton** was hailed as 'The Golden Voice of Two Continents'.

Comedian /singer **Reg Dixon's** (1915-1984) billing could either be "Confidentially" which was the titled of his signature tune or his catch phrase of 'Proper Poorly', something that Reg would often describe himself as being.

As heard on his popular radio series 'That's Life', **Al Read's** comedy approach was based around his great talent for observing other people's idiosyncrasies. Also used in his billing, his catch-phrase of 'Right Monkey' was at the time probably one of the most familiar in the country.

Jimmy Clitheroe would be billed as 'The Clitheroe Kid', which of course became the name of his popular radio series.

Born in Liverpool but living in Morecambe, **Albert Modley** was often billed as 'Lancashire's Favourite Comedian' alongside his well known saying '(It's) Grand To Be Daft' whilst also sometimes exclaiming "Eeh, I could just eat a nice meat pie!" Albert was also remembered for his comedy antics as a tram driver, complete with a picture of the front of a tram hung down in front of him on a curtain.

Billed alongside female comedienne **Hilda Baker's** name would be her familiar catch-phrase "She Knows Y'know" which she would use along with gestures towards her stooge Cynthia.

Turning from a dramatic operatic piece into funny one-liner, singer and comedienne **Joan Turner** would be billed with 'the voice of an Angel – the wit of a devil' or, alternatively, 'Operatic Mimicry'..

Another funny man, **Ken Platt's** (1921-1998) name would usually be followed by the words "I'll Not Take Me Coat Off" which usually preceded the rest of his catch-phrase "I'm Not Stopping'. Pint-sized **Charlie Drake's** (1925-2006) catchphrase was of course 'Hello My Darlings' and was consolidated when it became a popular song that he recorded.

Singer and comedian **Harry Secombe** usually had a customary 'Well Hello There' after his name. Tipping his hat, cockney comedian **Tommy Trinder** always signed off with his familiar catch-phrase 'You Lucky People'.

Singer **Frankie Vaughan** was usually billed as 'Mr. Moonlight' after of course his popular song "Give Me The Moonlight".

A comedian who could be pretty suggestive as well as quite looney, was **Max Wall** and in view of this received the billing of 'Irresponsible'.

Whilst everybody knew **Norman Evans** for his sketch 'Over The Garden Wall', his other billing was short & sweet with 'Good Evans'.

Following his rapid rise to fame, **Norman Wisdom** had quite a mouthful when billed as 'The Comedian that the Critics Made a Star Overnight'.

Reflecting their witty onstage repartee, comedy trio **The Allen Brothers & June** were billed as 'Two Sparks & A Flame'.

Also because of his quick sense of humour and delivery, northern comedian **Bill Waddington** (1916-2000) was either billed as 'Witty Willie' or 'Jester Wit'.

Also referring to his Northern humour, comedian **Sandy Lane** would have 'Yorkshire Relish', preceding his name. Backing up her name **Carroll Levis**' glamorous regular co-star **Violet Pretty** (1932) was also appropriately billed as 'irresistable' and also 'The TV Eyeful'. She later changed her name to **Ann Heywood** and pursued an acting career. Some of the lesser known acts also had their own tag-lines such as **Jimmy Gay** who had 'Putting the Gay in Paree' whilst black singing duo **Harriott & Evans** had 'Harmony in Sepia'. Being one of the many theatrical acrobatic acts **Felixio** sought after a little more individualism by billing himself under the more exotic title of 'Equilibrist'.

Many of the lesser known names also had their own 'Bill Matter', probably as a means to give them a bit more individuality or identity. Many of these were both quite curious and entertaining.

For whatever reason, **Ernest Arnley & Gloria Day** had 'Clean Crazy' after their names whilst **Dante** the magician had the magic words, 'Sim Sala Bim' after his.

Possibly following in the footsteps of Arthur English was **Scott Sanders** who was billed as 'The Last of the Barrow Boys'. Another comedian, **Norman Carrol** had an odd billing although probably true with 'Never 'Eard of Him'.

On similar lines was **Johnny Lockwood** (1920) whose billing of 'You've Never Heard Of Him – But You Will' was maybe another back-handed compliment. On the other hand, 'Too Funny For Words' was the billing that preceded

comedy act **Noberti** and would possibly invite some negative comments. Tall, lanky comedian **Donald B. Stuart** celebrated the fact with his billing of 'Variety's Longest Laugh'.

Still attempting to find fame, comedy duo **Morecambe & Wise** (real names John Eric Bartholomew, 1926-1984 and Ernest Wiseman, 1925-1999) were often at the bottom of the bill and were billed as simply 'Comedians' just to let everybody know what they were. one the silliest was 'Unknown to Millions' for which comedian **Reg Thompson** was rather unflatteringly billed as.

More curious bill matter goes with the strangely named act **Moke and Doke** with 'It's No Joke' after their name! Whatever they did, **Hall, Norman and Ladd** were billed as 'musical zombies' and just as bewildering, to conclude this chapter, bill matter for some of acts, without seeing them perform, certainly conjures up some intriguing images, as with; **Ron and Rita** - 'Comedy on the Slack Wire', **Charles Smart** 'With His Wonder Organ' and **Rex Roper and Maisie** 'With Their Ropes and Whips'! The mind boggles.

1   *Carroll Levis get an eyeful of Violet Pretty*
2   *A young Morecambe and Wise*

Onto Other Things

From their beginnings in variety, there were many, many names who would subsequently achieve further success of varying degrees and also as by way of another emerging talent.

Former variety star who has since become a long-established cast member of the popular Manchester-based soap Coronation Street is **Betty Driver**.(1920) Originally a singer with the big-band of Sid Phillip, Betty became a popular singer and comedienne. A familiar face on stage and television in the 50's she maybe remembered whilst singing she would make humorous gestures to the little pet dog she clutched under her arm.

In her portrayal of Betty Turpin in Coronation Street, Betty still retains some of her wonderful humour in the character.

In his role as comedian **Bill Waddington** was always quite bright and breezy offering non-stop laughter which was indeed a contrast to his more famous role of the starchy moaner Percy Sugden from TV's Coronation Street.

With a career that included both serious and comedy acting, **Bernard Miles** achieved great success and recognition as one of Britain's great actors that resulted in him being knighted for his work. However in the 50's he was regularly seen on stage and television in the guise of a west country farm yokel.

Personality singer Betty Driver is seen here with the vocal-instrumental group who will accompany her on a long tour of Germany, commencing in September. They comprise her husband, guitarist Wally Petersen; his two brothers Basil and Andy; and Betty's pianist Reg Hoskins.

1 Betty Driver   2 Mickie Most   3 Bernard Miles

Barry Took (1928-2002) would appear at the Empire as part of the Carroll Levis show, helping out as compere and telling funny gags. At the time he was also developing a career as a comedy script writer.

One half of 50's rock'n'roll duo The Most Brothers was **Mickie Most**. He got his start as one of the young talents to emerge from the famous Two I's Coffee Bar. In the late 50's/early 60's Most enjoyed some recording success in South Africa before returning to the UK and a brief run of solo recordings including "Mr. Porter" and "Sea Cruise". However he would achieve greater fame as independent record producer, working with such names as Herman's Hermits, Suzi Quatro and Smokie. He will also be remembered for his role as one of the, at times insensitive, judges on the 70's TV talent show 'New Faces'. The other Most Brother, **Alex Wharton** went onto half a brief solo career and recorded his version of the tragedy song "Teen Angel". He produced Ken Dodd's record of "Love Is Like A Violin" before he subsequently discovered The Moody Blues whom he managed. One time members of **Morton Fraser's Harmonica Gang**, **Don Paul**, **Gordon Mills**, **Ronnie Wells** went onto form pop vocal group The Viscounts whose records included Who Put The Bomp and Rockin' Little Angel and was part of Gene Vincent and Eddie Cochran's ill-fated tour of April 1960. Indian-born **Gordon Mills** (1935-1986) later went onto become manager of superstar Tom Jones and form his own record label MAM. Pianist **Dennis King** was the youngest brother in teenage act **The King Brothers**. Following a musical career onstage and on record, he would later go onto become a noted TV and film composer, provide theme tunes for a number of well-known television series like 'Lovejoy'. Another composer who went onto enjoy world fame was bandleader **John Barry**. As the arranger for Adam Faith's early hits, John also wrote the score for Adam's first film 'Beat Girl'. He then of course went on to compose the globally famous "James Bond Theme". His other successes included "Born Free", 'The Lion in Winter', 'Midnight Cowboy' and 'Somewhere In Time' amongst many others. Pianist with the JB7, **Les Reed** became a successful arranger and songwriter with such successes as "Delilah", "Hello Happiness" and "The Last Waltz" (co-written with Barry Mason) and "There's A Kind Of Hush" (with Geoff Stephens) and "It's Not Unusual" (with Gordon Mills).

Another young star of the 50's **Jim Dale** went onto find further success when his more humorous acting side came to the fore and he became one of the regular stars of the 'Carry On' films. He later found further success when he moved to Hollywood and appeared in a number of US comedy films.

Knockabout comedian **Norman Wisdom** became a tremendous box-office attraction with his hugely popular series of films which included 'Trouble In Store', 'The Square Peg', 'Follow A Star' and 'A Stitch In Time'. He later went on to become an acclaimed straight actor.. Camp comedian **Larry Grayson** (real name William Sulley White, 1923-1995) of course went onto become host of the popular TV show The Generation Game along with his catch-phrases like "shut that door" or "look at the muck in here"..

Two young starlets who appeared in the 1954 touring show: **Love from Judy** were **Miss June Whitfield** (1925) and **Miss Barbara Windsor**. At the time **June** was of course one of the familiar voices on the weekly radio comedy 'Take It From Here' alongside Jimmy Edwards and Dick Bentley. She later went onto become one of Britain's best loved comedy actresses appearing in the popular TV sit-coms 'Terry & June', 'Absolutely Fabulous' and 'Green, Green Grass' as well as one of the regular cast in the popular topical comedy radio show 'Hudd Lines'. **Barbara Windsor** (real name Barbara Ann Deeks, 1937) began as a young model progressing to stage and cabaret appearances and of course became one of the regular stars of the many 'Carry On' films. In them she was generally famous for her often-exposed chest which would often be the subject of a smutty one-liner. Although still with some of her brash cockney charm Barbara has since become known in her straighter acting role in the TV soap 'Eastenders'.

Former leader of The Vipers' Skiffle Group, **Wally Whyton** maybe remembered from the 60's when appeared on the children's TV show 'Five O'Clock Club' providing the voices for and talking to animal puppets Ollie Beak, Joe Crow, Spike McPike and Pussy Cat William. He then went onto record albums of children's songs and later became the 'voice of British country music when he presented the Radio 2 series 'Country Club'

Comedy actor **Bernard Bresslaw** was another regular in the 'Carry On' films. But prior to this it's a little known fact that because of his stature, he was chosen to play the creature in Hammer Films 1957 revival of Frankenstein, before the part was given to Christopher Lee.

By the 50's. Comedian **Benny Hill** was becoming a popular face on TV and consolidated this with appearances on stage. In the 70's and 80's he would of course become famous for his numerous series of 'Benny Hill Shows' which subsequently achieved cult status. This would probably be due to the fact that he would usually feature a bevy of glamorous and often scantily-clad, female beauties together with the large amounts of sexual innuendo incorporated into his various comedy and musical routines.

Comedienne **Hylda Baker** had been a regular favourite on TV through the 50's and 60's and in the early 70's made a comeback when she was given the starring role in the popular ITV sitcom "Nearest & Dearest'. alongside another stage veteran **Jimmy Jewel**. The two played brother and sister Nellie and Ely Pledge who ran the family pickling firm Pledges Pickles.

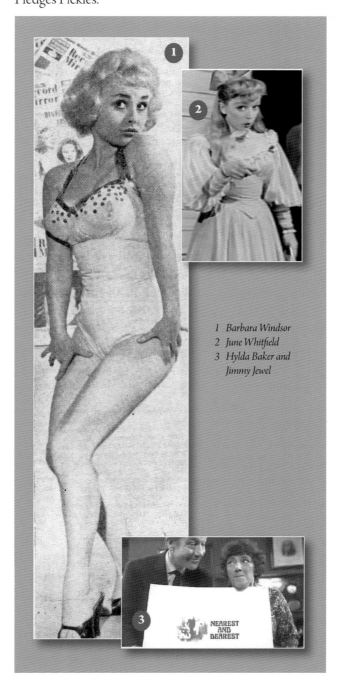

1 Barbara Windsor
2 June Whitfield
3 Hylda Baker and
   Jimmy Jewel

Famous as a singer, crooner **Jimmy Young** of course went onto enjoy further popularity and status after he'd stopped singing. Between the late 60's to the late 90's he became recognised as a top radio presenter and after his own successful career on record, he found playing other people's records quite amusing. Also talking about the various topics of the day his daily programme on Radio 2 became an important voice.

Following on from his success on record **Frankie Vaughan's** career would progress to seeing have a brief career in films. This began in the comedy film "Ramsbottom Rides Again" co-starring with Arthur Askey. His first major film was the drama 'These Dangerous Years', followed by 'Wonderful Things', 'The Heart Of A Man' and Let's Make Love'. In the latter film he co-starred with Marilyn Monroe who it was reported, had 'designs' on Frankie, but were declined in view of his devotion to his wife Stella.

Rubber-necked **Nat Jackley** would also be billed as such when he made a small but memorable appearance in the Beatles film 'Magical Mystery Tour'. Nat would go on further into acting with cameo roles on TV including one of the 'Minder' episodes and other TV dramas including Shakespeare's 'Midsummer Night's Dream..

King of the wide-boys **Arthur English** went onto become a character actor, with his most well known role being that as Mr. Harman, the store caretaker in the comedy series 'Are You Being Served?'

One time comedian **Dickie Dawson** is remembered for his role as Private Pete Newkirk in the 1960's US TV comedy Wartime series 'Hogan's Heroes'. Years later he re-emerged on screen again as the obnoxious TV show host in the **Arnold Schwartzenegger** film 'Running Man'.

The sharp young comic who appeared at the Empire was **Des O'Connor** who later became a household name with his TV chat shows as well as hosting a revived version of Take Your Pick and more recently Countdown. He was the butt of many a **Morecambe and Wise** joke.

1 Arthur English *2 Bruce Forsyth*

Back in the 1950's **Roy Castle** was one of the gormless looking stooges in comedian Jimmy James' act. As a performer in his own right, he developed into a talented singer, tap dancer and trumpeter and went onto become a successful television and cabaret entertainer. In the 1980's he became a familiar sight on TV as the host of BBC television popular 'Record Breakers' show. A great campaigner against smoking in public, Roy bravely died whilst suffering from cancer in September 1994.

Combining singing, dancing, piano-playing and comedy **Bruce Forsyth** (real name Bruce Joseph Forsyth Johnson, 1928) emerged as a most versatile performer early on. This of course has resulted in him enjoying a long and very successful career on stage and television. It was as the compere of the weekly TV spectacular 'Sunday Night At The London Palladium' that his career took off. With this he also became well-known for his catch-phrase "I'm In Charge" which was the title of one of his over-looked recordings. From there he went onto host other popular television shows like 'The Generation Game', 'Bruce's Play Your Cards Right' and a stint as a comedy actor in the super-market sitcom, 'Slinger's Day' whilst more recently 'Strictly Come Dancing' have all today made Bruce a showbiz institution.

Another entertainer who emerged as something of a new-wave comic back in the 1950's is **Ken Dodd** (1927) Today he is of course a show business legend. Following in the footsteps of other fellow Liverpool comics (Rob Wilton, Tommy Handley, Arthur Askey and Ted Ray), Ken maintains his popularity both onstage and television as a very funny comedian. In doing so, he continues follow his personal ambition of appearing at every theatre in England, (although we wonder if this will include The Lantern Theatre?)

Someone else who later went on to make a name for herself (in fact more than one) was one-time Empire usherette **Audrey Middleton** (1937) from Page Hall, Sheffield. Working at the theatre she naturally met many of the stars, one of whom was singer **Yana** and the two became friends. Another artist that Audrey became very friendly with was singer **Alex Wharton**, of singing duo **The Most Brothers**. Although she'd recently married soldier Alan Bradshaw, Audrey ran away to London to be with Wharton with whom she became pregnant but sadly miscarried. She became a night-club singer and also appeared in the horror film 'Flesh & The Fiends'. Through impresario Larry Parnes. Audrey was renamed **Lady Lee** and in the 60's recorded for Decca and would also become the partner of singer Billy Fury. She then later became the wife of zany yet troubled D.J. Kenny Everett and today is known as Lee Everett-Alkin after marrying actor John Alkin and today sells recipes for chilli sauces and relishes and which is a far cry from Page Hall and the Sheffield Empire.

Empire
THEATRE SHEFFIELD

chapter six

The Final Curtain and Beyond

Chapter Six

Final Curtain & Beyond

Remembering the last show at The Empire

By the late fifties, the world of entertainment was changing and television (or 'goggle-box' as it was known) had taken its toll on many of the old theatres as audiences could watch their favourite personalities and variety shows, etc. in the comfort of their own home. The Queen's coronation in 1953 had been a major factor in the rise of TV sets being purchased and in 1955 ITV, or 'commercial' television had added to it's pulling power. Reflecting this, the Empire was one of the theatres that suffered as audiences dwindled and with its somewhat grimy and battle-scarred frontage, the theatre conceded defeat and staged its final production on Saturday 2nd May, 1959. It starred comedian **Albert**

1 *The Old Empire Theatre, looking forlorn, just before its demolition*
2 *Albert Modley ponders over the Empires final closure*

Modley in a variety show titled 'On With The Modley' sponsored by the Smedleys Food Company. To get tickets, labels from two Smedley's tins had to be taken to the box office a few days before the show. Therefore, in order to get tickets, did people have to watch their 'peas and queues'?! This then entitled ticket-holders to sit anywhere in the theatre, including the Royal Boxes. Despite an obvious air of despondency, Sheffielders packed the theatre in recognition of its significance, for the last show, and probably because it was free!

John Ward; "I remember the last show because my grandmother had a corner shop on Milton St/Hanover St selling groceries and she removed the paper wrappings off several tins of Smedleys Peas which could be exchanged for tickets to the show. I went with mother, grandmother and myself for free."

As always, Maurice Newton and the Empire orchestra began the evening's entertainment and although he did it with a heavy heart, Maurice still managed to give the audience his familiar 'Newtonian' smile as he acknowledged the audience's applause.

Philip Depledge also has a special memory of the night; "I attended the last show which was sponsored by Smedley's Peas as my Father Harold Depledge was employed by Nichols, Johnson and Bingham of Shalesmoor and he received tickets for the show. He took along my mother, brother and myself along with my uncle Reg Depledge, his wife and daughter. Part way through the show a competition took place and my uncle and two others were called up onto the stage to take part. They each were given ping-pong balls to throw into a metal bucket. My uncle was the only one to be successful and won the prize of a refrigerator full of Smedley's frozen foods. This was amazing as he was the only one in the family to own such a wonder as a 'fridge' and his only worry was where could it go in their small house!"

At the end of the show **Albert Modley** made a moving speech and the following day had his picture (left) taken inside the Empire, contemplating its future.

Two weeks later the fixtures and fittings of the old theatre went up for auction. 1,400 seats went for 2/- and 6/- each (10p and 30p), The 25 foot long counter from the stalls bar was sold for £14.10s. 0d. (£14.50p). However, after the three hour auction, many of the items enjoyed a new lease of life in some of the remaining theatres. Backstage, the dressing rooms, which had been named after other great theatres; Tivoli, Palladium, Empire and Hippodrome, were silent and empty.

The demolition of the Empire certainly struck a sad note with many of it's former patrons. **John Ward**; "My lasting memory was one Sunday morning when I went down and stood just off Union St for about 8 hours watching a crane with ball and chain swinging into the Empire and knocking it down, even at the age of 11 I thought it was a sin, it broke my heart." **Paul Walshaw**; "It was a sad day when the theatre closed; as a city centre worker I remember that the demolition seemed to take ages to complete." As indeed it seemed for many Sheffielders. Located on a prime city centre site, it was only a matter of two months before the demolition men moved in to start work and two months later in July The Empire was just a memory and replaced with shops, which are still on the site where the Empire Theatre stood.

1   The Old Empire Theatre being demolished

2   The Corner of Charles Street & Union Street today, supplementing the definite shortage of offices and shops in Sheffield

The Old Empire Theatre, bottom left of the picture. Pinstone Street, Charles Street and the Salvation Army Citadel can all be picked out from this aerial photograph.

London Connection

In many of the Empire's programmes there were also adverts for some of the shows that were playing that week at London theatres that belonged to the same management group. These included **The London Palladium**, **London Hippodrome** and **The Prince Of Wales**. Once again these bills were very interesting, showing details of a variety of shows starring more popular names.

The Palladium (*two programmes pictured left*) was of course Moss Empire's most prestigious venue and still enjoys world acclaim today. Some of it's shows of the 50's would feature names like **Danny Kaye, Gracie Fields, Ted Ray, Norman Wisdom, Ruby Murray, "Mr. Pastry" (Richard Hearn)** and **Dickie Valentine**.

The Hippodrome tended to concentrate on stage plays featuring such actors as such as **Ian Carmichael, Diana Churchill, Anton Walbrook, Evelyn Laye, Bernard Lee** and **Nigel Stock**.

The Prince Of Wales (*poster pictured below*) presented some of the more 'glamour' presentations with shows like the Folies Bergere revue of **"Paris To Piccadilly"**, **"Pardon My French"** and **"Paris By Night"** starring a host of names from variety.

Two London Palladium programmes

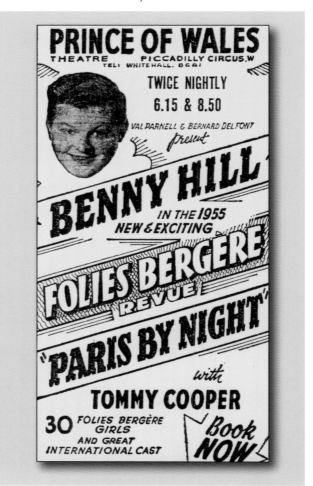

Four London Hippodrome posters

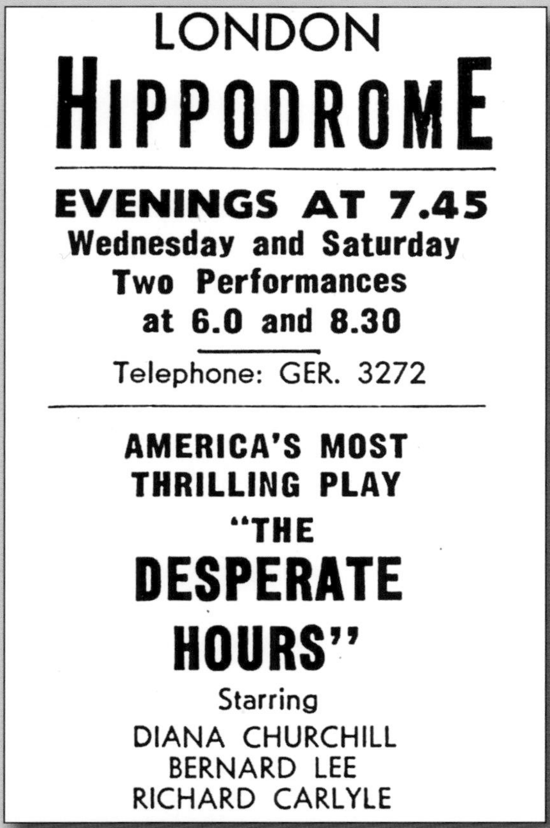
LONDON
HIPPODROME
EVENINGS AT 7.45
Wednesday and Saturday
Two Performances
at 6.0 and 8.30
Telephone: GER. 3272
AMERICA'S MOST
THRILLING PLAY
"THE
DESPERATE
HOURS"
Starring
DIANA CHURCHILL
BERNARD LEE
RICHARD CARLYLE

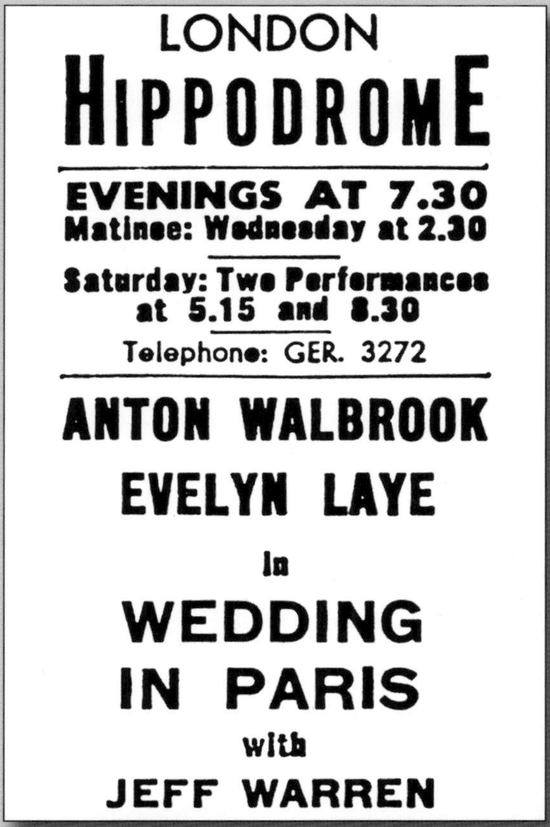
LONDON
HIPPODROME
EVENINGS AT 7.30
Matinee: Wednesday at 2.30
Saturday: Two Performances
at 5.15 and 8.30
Telephone: GER. 3272
ANTON WALBROOK
EVELYN LAYE
in
WEDDING
IN PARIS
with
JEFF WARREN

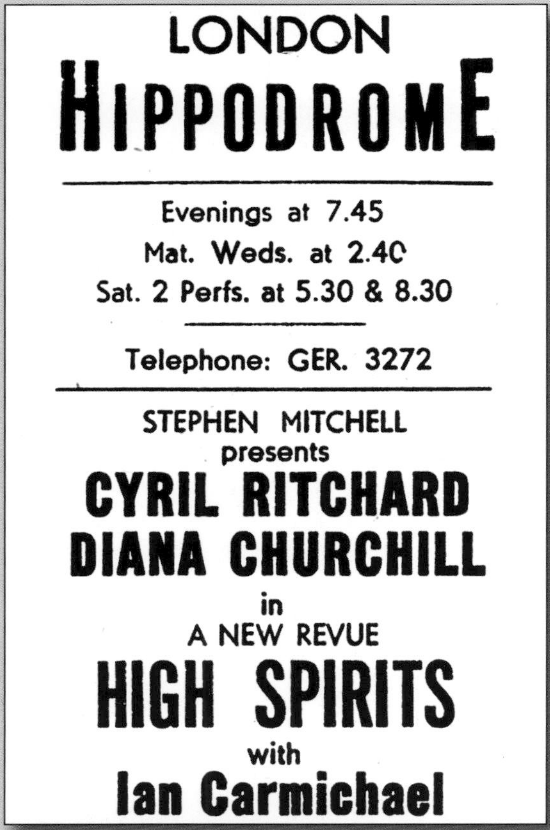
LONDON
HIPPODROME
Evenings at 7.45
Mat. Weds. at 2.40
Sat. 2 Perfs. at 5.30 & 8.30
Telephone: GER. 3272
STEPHEN MITCHELL
presents
CYRIL RITCHARD
DIANA CHURCHILL
in
A NEW REVUE
HIGH SPIRITS
with
Ian Carmichael

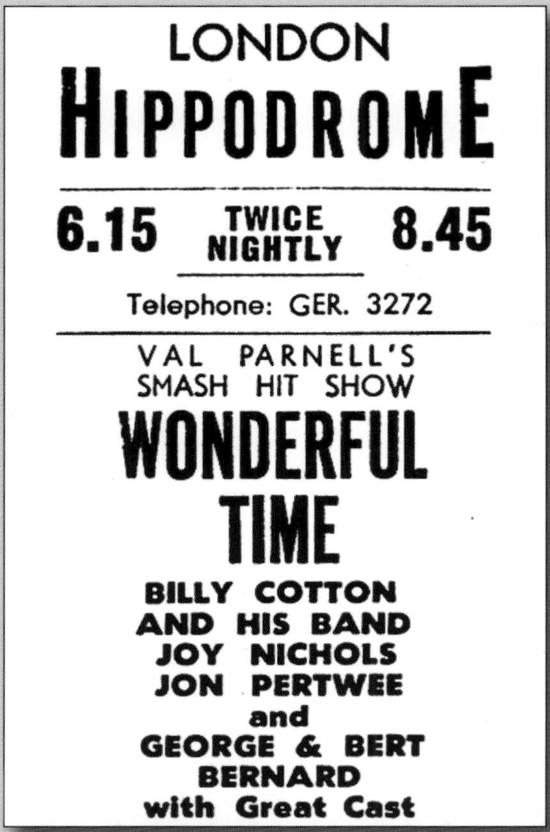
LONDON
HIPPODROME
6.15 TWICE NIGHTLY 8.45
Telephone: GER. 3272
VAL PARNELL'S
SMASH HIT SHOW
WONDERFUL
TIME
BILLY COTTON
AND HIS BAND
JOY NICHOLS
JON PERTWEE
and
GEORGE & BERT
BERNARD
with Great Cast

Moss & Stringfellow

The London Hippodrome was another of Moss's, venues, again designed by theatre architect, Frank Matcham. It was built for circus and variety and had a somewhat breathtaking entrance which was through a bar set out as a ships saloon. The performances took place on a proscenium stage and for aquatic performances it had an area that contained a 230 ft tank containing 100,000 gallons of water. The tank also featured numerous fountains as well as facilities for boats. Shows included acts with elephants, horses, polar bears and seals.

In the 1950's, many up and coming actors and actresses who went on to become stars of 1950's TV programs would appear at The Hippodrome as can be seen on the old theatre bills. These included such as Jon Pertwee who went onto become Dr Who and Bernard Lee who played M, in eleven James Bond films. The famous actress Diana Churchill, who was not as many people think Winston Churchill's, daughter.

In 1958 it became the Talk of the Town and featured such international artists as Frank Sinatra, Sammy Davis, Judy Garland, Lulu, Tom Jones amongst many other famous artists

1983 saw another connection between the Moss Theatre chain and Sheffield transpire by way of the flamboyant Sheffield club-owner **Peter Stringfellow** (1940) Sheffield's very own entrepreneur looked over the venue although he was initially put off by the rundown condition of the venue. However, the more Peter looked into the history of this old theatre the more he was drawn to it and the possibility of how he could keep the theatre alive. Fascinated by its history as the Hippodrome, with its maze of tunnels beneath the floor which were known as the elephant walk and the huge water tank fed by the underground River Cranbourne. He was also equally drawn to Moss's own fascinating life and career and could see similar parallels to his own.

Peter spent 3.5 million renovating the place with a state of the art lighting rig costing 1 million. It reverted back to its original name of the Hippodrome, after Peter, had a dream in which he was stood looking up at the old Talk of the Town sign which fell down revealing the original Hippodrome sign behind it, so regaining its original name.

Peter Stringfellow signing the Mojo Book

chapter seven

Sources

Chapter Seven

Sources

Acknowledgement to the following sources of reference

The Lost Theatres Of Sheffield
Bryen D. Hillerby, Wharncliffe Publishing, 1999

Sheffield Newspapers

T'owd Locals
J R Wrigley, Youbooks.co.uk Publishing, 2009

A Pub On Every Corner
Douglas Lamb, Hallamshire Press, 1996

Not Like A Proper Job
Martin Lilleker & John Firminger,
Juma Publishing, 2001

The Sheffield Chronicles
JP Bean, D&D Publications 2008

First Hits
Brian Henson & Colin Morgan, Boxtree
Publishing, 1989

Guinness Book Of Hit Singles
Joe & Tim Rice, Paul Gambaccini & Mike Read,
Guinness Superlatives Ltd, 1983

New Record & Show Mirror
1956 - 1959

Disc
1958 – 1959

Seats in All Parts
Leslie Frost, Magik Enterprises 1986

New Musical Express
1954 - 1959

Thanks for the Memories
Leslie Frost, Magik Enterprises 1988

Halfway To Paradise
Spencer Leigh & John Firminger, Finbarr 1996

King of Clubs
Peter Stringfellow with Fiona Lafferty, 1996.

Reminiscenses of Sheffield
by R E Leader (1896)

**Commonwealth War Graves Commission
The Blitz Then & Now. Vol 1-3.**
After the Battle Publications

Musical Opinion 1900 -1909
(private collection)

A Directory of Sheffield 1787
(authors collection)

Kellys Directory's Sheffield 1954 -59
(authors collection)

The Restless Generation
Pete Frame
Rogan House 2007

Shakin' All Over
Spencer Leigh,
Radio Merseyside, Radio Series 1983

Also thanks to the following
Vivian Davidsen, (nee Mihailovits)
Eric Kalman
Judd Newton
Margaret Hobson
Bob Davis
Martin Dawes (Sheffield Newspapers)
Elaine Marsh
Jack Wrigley

Limited Edition Book

The following list is of subscribers who wanted to be part of our
Limited Edition Collectors Copy of **"Curtain Up at the Empire"**

Every publication of the special edition will be signed and personally numbered
by the authors **John Firminger and Dave Manvell** .
It will also be recognised by its own Limited Edition, Sheffield Star, Cover

Pauline Webster

J Ward

Vi Levick

Tony Medlicott

Mr Cantrell

Steven William Hobson

Mr Joyce Mappin

Iris Janiszewski

Ann Chesney

Mrs Jean Warburton

George Humberstone

Robert Lawrence Pashley

David Bartles

Sarah Woodhead

Mrs Freada Williams

Stewart Howson

Kathleen Swift

Terry Jackson

Bryan H Barrett

Mary Eastwood

John Wheelhouse

Anthony D Barker

Sylvia Elliott

Margaret and Eric Bearman

Mary Haigh Glover

Mr Jeremy H Crawshaw

Raymond Sanderson

Karl D Halliday

Kathleen Elaine Rhodes

Leonard Forrester

Alice Harrison

Patricia Levesley

R L Annible

Joan

Colin Scott

James Larkin

Mrs Ruby Robertson

Sylvia Mawhood

Philip Depledge

Dorothy Stephenson

Reginald George Parsisson

Jack Birkinshaw
(Happy Birthday)

Maureen Watson

Robert Michael Prestwood

Trevor Yeardley

H N Allott

Albert E Shaw

Sheila Lowis

Geoff Garbett

Brian Reaney

Patricia

Michael J Waterhouse

Don Hall

Derek Tingle

Gerald Hobson

Cyril Moore

June Kirkland

Anne Kerrison

Dot and Shead

Frank R Chadwick

Glenice

June Brown

Noreen Driver

Frank Phillips

Nancy Grayson

Tony Purt

Amy Hannah Thompson

Michael Liversidge

Gary Mackender

J R Wrigley

John Burland

Abigail Emma Liversidge

Steven Hird

Edna Hird

Terry & Marie France

Lionel Mackender

David Drabble

Another Fine Mess